# DREAMBIGGER
## LIVEBETTER

# DREAMBIGGER
# LIVEBETTER

## Donna Palm

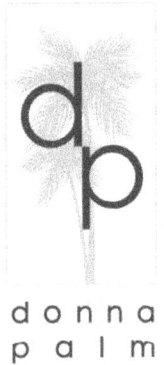

donna palm

Published 2013 by Donna Palm

Three Palms In Paradise Inc.

Dream Bigger Live Better
Copyright 2013
© Donna Palm/Three Palms in Paradise Inc.

Hard-cover ISBN: 978-0-9910948-1-3
Soft-cover ISBN: 978-0-9910948-0-6
Library of Congress Control Number: 2013954864
Printed in Sarasota, Florida, The United States of America

*All Rights Reserved.*
No part of this publication may be reproduced, sold, or distributed without prior written permission from the publisher and copyright holder.

Submit permission requests to:
info@donnapalm.com

Three Palms in Paradise Inc.
P.O. Box 155
Laurel, FL 34272

www.DonnaPalm.com

*This book is dedicated to
all those who dare to dream…*

## Table of Contents

Chapter 1 .................................................................. 1
Blueprint Your Dreams

Chapter 2 ................................................................ 51
What Are You Waiting For?

Chapter 3 ................................................................ 93
Rescue Yourself

Chapter 4 .............................................................. 117
What Does It Take To Be A Success?

Chapter 5 .............................................................. 153
Relationships Matter

Chapter 6 .............................................................. 185
Time Is Of The Essence

# Preface

There is an old, yet familiar story thought to be originated by an entomologist in Germany. After conducting intensive observations and extensive calculations, he came to the conclusion that due to its size and weight, the bumblebee should not be able to fly.

**Good Thing No One Told the Bumble Bee!**

In my dreams I want to be a breath of fresh air, inspire others to follow their dreams and live the most fulfilling life possible. I want others to believe in their own possibilities without self-imposed limits; and to see for themselves their unlimited potential. ~Donna Palm - Mission Statement

Don't waste time living a mundane and unfulfilled life; watching life go by without taking the initiative to fulfill your dreams and not believing in your own potential. Life is short, so we have to cram everything in before we leave to go to the next phase of this world or this existence. I spent the first part of my life not knowing what I wanted to do or how to pursue it. I felt like I was in training everyday of my life, building strength and muscle for the future. I've come to learn the harder the ride, the stronger the muscles. You don't build muscles by taking the easy way out. I want to lead others to find joy. Remember, you can't have success without some failure, and you can't have success if you never try.

# Introduction

Throughout my life, one question has repeatedly been asked of me no matter where I was or what I was doing. People have asked me over and over again, "How in the world do you do it?"

'How do you as a single mom run a business, take care of a house, haul the kids to baseball and soccer, etc.?'

'How do you pick up everything you own, move to a place where you know absolutely no one and start a brand new life?'

'How do you find the confidence to redesign your life and follow your dreams?'

'How in the world do you do it?'

Well, to all of you who have asked me these questions over the years, here it is. I have finally written the instruction manual. This book includes several popular and well-known insights to life. Many of you will probably recognize them. However, what this book also includes are many things you have not heard before - things that I have developed over years of life experience. I only wish I had this book to follow when I started on this journey. Luckily, it is never too late. It is my desire to inspire all of you to follow your life's dreams by following the Blueprint I have laid out for you in this book.

Following the Blueprint, you should be able to accomplish anything your heart desires. It is important to take the time to do the exercises so you can completely enjoy the fulfillment of your potential. As you read further into the book you will understand why. Together, we will consider the ups and downs we all go through in life. We will discuss successes and failures and what to do when we have fallen into a "hole." Life is not perfect and neither are we. However, by following the Blueprint and reading and implementing the teachings and concepts in this book, you will have the confidence and ability to turn things around and take a "Do-Over" at will.

Everything you need is here; the rest is up to you.

**DREAM**BIGGER
**LIVE**BETTER

# CHAPTER 1

## BLUEPRINT YOUR DREAMS

*"Live for today, plan for tomorrow, remember yesterday."*
~Donna Palm

Who am I to tell you anything about being successful?

I'm Donna Palm. I've spent my entire life working to get to this point. I'm writing this book and sharing my story because if I can accomplish my goals, so can you.

To be honest, if you had asked me 20 years ago about being an author or successful entrepreneur, I would have shaken my head and laughed away the possibility of such an absurd idea. Unfortunately, like so many other people, I bought into the lies and negativity of Dream Stealers who didn't see anything else for my life, other than what was right in front of them at the moment. Neither they—nor I—could see past my present situation to imagine or envision a more vibrant and successful future.

I used to be uncomfortable with my own story—how I started, mistakes I made, and failures I faced. But, I'm not anymore. Because I've learned that it's not how you start the race, it's all about how you finish. And even though I'm not done yet, I feel really good about where things are now and where they're headed in the future.

Borrowing inspiration from the famous comedic Marx brothers, I ask: "Who are you gonna believe; me or your lying eyes?" Too many of us believe our "lying eyes" and accept the premise that what we see before us is what will always be upon us. And that absolutely does not have to be the case.

We all have the right—and the responsibility—to map out a life that is worthy of living. I call it a Blueprint.

## Blueprint Your Dreams and Your Life

*"You design your house, you design your business, you design your clothes, and you design your style; so why not take time to design your life?"* ~Donna Palm

Your life—much like any building, home, or office—has a blueprint design for its structure, style, and purpose. There is a foundation, along with infrastructure, and an overall plan that tells the world why it exists. Your life too has a purpose, so it's important to blueprint your dreams to ensure the successful construction of a well-lived life.

It's often said, that if you don't know where you're going, any road will take you there. Having a blueprint for your life and for your dreams will keep you from wandering aimlessly toward accomplishing nothing – and put you on the fast track to seeing your dreams come true. Your life's blueprint is the instruction manual or user's guide for constructing the best version of yourself. It's the roadmap for life's journey that ultimately leads to the fulfillment of your dreams.

Where are you going? How will you get there? Who's going with you? How will you know when you arrive? I've learned that asking the right questions is the answer.

Admittedly, no matter how great a blueprint you have, life can still hit you squarely between the eyes and knock you flat on your back.

I grew up in Chicago, Illinois, during the height of the manufacturing boom. I was adopted into a middle-class family who lived in the suburbs and spent my adolescent and teenage years making a blueprint for the life I wanted to live.

In 1982, I graduated from Montini High School, and that same year, I also graduated from LaGrange School of Cosmetology. I attended high school full time while completing cosmetology school nights, weekends, and over the summer of my junior and senior years. Being a licensed cosmetologist paved the way for me to venture into entrepreneurship and own a hair salon named Mane Design for more than 5 years. During that time, I also worked as a veterinary technician. Clearly, I was driven – even as a teen.

In 1986, at age 21, I found myself living in my car—a Datsun 200SX—with my dog Jake, a 100-pound black and rust Doberman Pinscher. Although I was working four jobs, seven days a week at the time; sometimes 20 hour days, supporting myself and trying to make ends meet, I still ended up "homeless" for a while because no apartment complex wanted to allow Jake on the premises. It's interesting how the tough lean years build the most character on the journey of success. Every now and then I think back to those days of working as a cashier, inventory stocker, veterinary technician, and hair stylist... all at the same time. That's when I developed a serious work ethic that would take me very far in life.

In 1987, I was accepted into the International Brotherhood of Electrical Workers Apprenticeship program in Joliet, Illinois. I was only the third woman to be accepted out of more than 1,500 men. The apprenticeship required 5 years of classroom training and 5 years of on-the-job training. Upon graduating, I was immediately promoted into supervision. You would never know just by looking at me that I was an industrial electrician constructing oil refineries, chemical plants, nuclear plants, and steel mills. Running my own business and working as an electrician helped hone my work ethic. It was not unusual during those days to put in 12-hour days and 84-hour work weeks. By my mid-30s, I was exhausted and burnt out – wishing and hoping for a different outcome for my life. By then, I had been married and divorced twice – definitely not what I had planned.

In 2000, after my second divorce was finalized, I was introduced to the life, challenges, and experiences of being a single parent. At that time, my children were 2 and 3 years old. I had grown weary of the cold winters in Illinois, the long hours at work, and living someone else's life instead of the life I had dreamed of. I decided that things had to change. In 2002, I blueprinted my new life; and moved to Florida to realize my dreams and begin anew. As you see, I've come a long way. No matter what roadblocks you've faced, it's never too late to start over.

Throughout my career, I've been a lot of clichés: Single mom. Working woman. Homeless person. Divorced parent. Struggling entrepreneur. And for a while, one of the only women among hundreds of men in the local union for the International Brotherhood of Electrical Workers. After putting in the necessary work and paying my dues, I earned a few more titles. Real Estate Agent. Real Estate Broker. After that, I became a business owner and success story, owning two very successful RE/MAX offices in Florida.

It's fair to say that my success has surprised a lot of people – sometimes, even me. That's the reason I decided to write this book, because so many people I've met and worked with along the way wanted to know how I did it. How did I as a single divorced mom—on my own—change my entire life for the better? Most of them want to know how they can do it too. My purpose is to share my experiences and expertise so that as many other people as possible can achieve their dreams and goals, using my story as their inspiration. No one has a monopoly on success. If you're willing to put in the work, you can make your dreams come true. Anything I can do, you can do too. Despite being a single mom and having to live in my car for a while, "I don't look like what I've been through."

It would be accurate to say that most of the people in my life have little to no idea of the things that I have achieved or experienced. Most don't know what I have been through in order to get where I am now. There are a lot of things in my life that I haven't shared with many people, so a lot of individuals who read this book are going to be really surprised. What's not surprising is that the same principles that applied to me apply to everyone else too. If my readers will follow these straightforward and simple success principles, they can realize the same types of results for their lives.

## You Need to Know Where You are Going Before You Can Get There

*"In life, you don't need to know all of the answers, you just need to know where to find them."* ~Donna Palm

When it comes to pursuing any goal, dream, or vision, it's important to Begin With the End in Mind. You have to know where you're going in order to figure out the best way to get there. Or as people often say, "If you don't know where you're going, how will you know when you get there?"

Concerning my own life's blueprint, I think of it in terms of establishing crystal clear goals so that my mind comprehends them and knows how to make them materialize. In 2002 when I decided as a single mom to move someplace warm, I didn't just simply jump into the car and head toward Florida. I made a blueprint plan. First, I thought about all the warm places I could choose to live: Hawaii, Arizona, California, and Florida. Then I decided I needed to be somewhere that had easy access back home to Chicago so I could visit my family and my parents. I also determined that I wanted to be near the water. My plan had a purpose, and its purpose was to outline what I wanted and how I planned to get what I wanted. My blueprint included all the things that were important: the must-haves. Once I wrote down my wants and needs, it was easy to visualize my plan and make an informed decision about my next steps. I decided to move to Florida because it fit the blueprint for my dreams.

A lot of people would find uprooting their family and lifestyle and moving to a brand new state with absolutely no job, family, friends, or connections to be crazy. Not me! It made perfect sense and I was 100 percent certain that things would work out for the best because I had a blueprint. In my life, for some reason, I've achieved just about everything I've ever put my mind to. Sometimes it was quite difficult and sometimes things came relatively easy. But the one consistent factor for my results was the effort I put into achieving my goal. Any time I put in wishy-washy energy or wishy-washy work, I received wishy-washy results. However, whenever I was really determined that I wanted something or wanted to do something, if I put solid energy into it, did solid research, and made a solid plan... I achieved everything I wanted. If I believed in something and worked toward it, I usually achieved success. If I did not believe in something or only gave it a fraction of my attention, that's when I did not get the results I wanted or expected.

Looking back over my life, I can honestly say: If I had known then what I know now, I would have saved a lot of time, energy, frustration, and agony. I wish I'd had this book back when I started. Luckily, for those of you reading this book now, you can learn from my mistakes and the mistakes of others, because life is too short to make all the mistakes yourself.

So, why I did succeed?

I believe the keys to my success as a student, apprentice, electrician, business owner, parent, real estate broker, consultant, actress, and model have been the combination of focus, excitement, and determination to work my plan and blueprint my dreams.

Just like a blueprint is a drawing or schematic of what the finished structure will look like, you can create a drawing of what your successful life looks like. Make a solid written plan. Use pictures, or images, or even an online scrapbook service to put together the picture of your ideal life. Make sure that the images tell the story of how you get from where you are to where you want to be. Put your blueprint in an easy-to-find place where you can quickly access and reference it to prevent going off course.

You only live once, so you have to cram in all your dreams to make sure you live out your full potential. That is one of the reasons I've had so many careers, because I can't imagine doing the same thing my entire life. No matter how many goals or dreams you have, the key to accomplishing them all is having a blueprint plan. Just like architects, engineers, and contractors follow blueprints to construct buildings, you can follow this blueprint to build the life you want.

## Dreams and Plans

*"Too many of us are not living our dreams because we're too busy living our fears."*

When we are young, our dreams are so big and so exciting that we can barely wait to grow up to create and live out those dreams. During adolescence and young adulthood, our potential and abilities seem limitless. Think about how you used to be. You were fearless, and so was I. We could dream, we could fly, we could soar to the moon solely off of imagination. Because we did not know fear, life did not get in our way. Anything was possible. Sometimes we need to rekindle those dreams and start believing again in the possibility of our own unlimited potential. The only way to get those dreams in gear is to have a plan or blueprint. We need to create goals and follow through with them. Our environment, our peers, who and what we are surrounded by affect us. Those things can affect us in a positive way or in a negative way. We must realize that the components of our surroundings can create our dreams or steal our dreams.

I believe that our dreams are simply a subconscious extension of who we really are. Think about it. How can you possibly dream or envision something that isn't inherently a part of your personality? That's why people say things like, "If you can see it, you can be it." And that's why phrases like "see it to believe it" or "think your way rich" make sense. Dreams are intangible blueprints, and dreaming is the origination of manifestation. In other words, once you can dream of something, the next step is to begin taking the necessary steps to turn that dream into reality.

In my opinion, Dreamers are the only real Doers!

Famous animator, storyteller, entrepreneur, and "Imagineer" (fusion of imagination and engineer) Walt Disney dreamed an impossible dream and literally brought it to life on the small screen, the big screen, and in theme parks that draw millions of visitors each year. Disney dreamed a dream so big that there was room enough for all of us to share in his dream. Are you dreaming big enough so that someone other than you can benefit too?

When Walt Disney looked out into what was then a vast swampland in central Florida, he didn't see what everyone else saw. Disney was able to see past the swamp and into the future. He was able to envision what was possible, not just what was visible.

"One of the greatest dreamers of our time was Walt Disney. Did you know he created the first sound cartoon, the first all-color cartoon, and the first animated feature length motion picture? Not only was he not afraid to dream, he was not afraid to walk those dreams into reality." [www.DisneyDreamer.com]

**Beware of the Dream Stealers!**

Beware! Dream Stealers come in all ages, sizes, shapes, and forms. The problem with most Dream Stealers is that we often don't recognize them until it's too late, because they are cleverly disguised as parents, teachers, coaches, and friends—people whom we expect to automatically be on our side; encouraging us, rooting for us, and cheering us on.

Dream Stealers are the people who intentionally or unintentionally discourage us from pursuing what they feel is too lofty a goal. Often well-meaning, Dream Stealers are infamous for seeing the glass as "half empty" and finding all the reasons that something cannot be done. They are easily identifiable by their speech, frequently using pessimistic words and phrases like: never, no one, impossible, can't, unlikely, and we've never done it that way before.

Don't be a Dream Stealer and don't listen to Dream Stealers.

A very close friend of mine was in college in the 1970s and desperately wanted to become a teacher, at a time when most teachers were women. He was told by his professor that he would never get a job as a teacher because he was a man. His college professor—a trusted advisor and mentor—inadvertently stole his dream. I'm certain the professor meant well and possibly thought he was doing my friend a favor. But that's the danger of dream stealers. By the time we recognize them for who and what they are, it's often too late. Unfortunately, my friend listened to him and to this day still wishes he had become a teacher.

We have to be careful that we don't steal other people's dreams as well. Sometimes just the slightest bit of negativity or doubt can ruin a dream for someone else if their dream is new, young, or not yet firmly rooted. Let's make sure that in our desire to help or warn those we care about, we don't accidentally extinguish the flames of promise and potential. It is sad and shameful that sometimes people in authority or people who are looked up to can have such a negative effect on others, especially children, teens, and young adults who are ripe with hope and optimism. We have to be careful not to allow the cynicism of our past hurts, failures, or disappointments to douse the hopes of the next generation. Keep that in mind.

Dream Stealers aren't always other people on the outside. Sometimes the Dream Stealer lies within. Our own fears, insecurities, and anxieties can become overwhelming to the extent that we listen and obey those inner voices that tell us we can't do something. We also need to be careful as we get older that we don't start losing our dreams because of life circumstances or because a lot of time passes and it looks like our dreams aren't going to come true. Somehow throughout the ups and downs, and trials and tribulations of life, many of us have forgotten our dreams. We have been distracted, disappointed, discouraged, or believed other people who have lost their dreams - and then said ours were not possible either. There's a great African proverb that says, "If there is no enemy within, the enemy without can do you no harm." Isn't that an awesome expression? Once we defeat the Dream Stealer within, we can conquer or overcome any Dream Stealers we may encounter throughout our lives. Here's some more good news... your dreams don't have an expiration date. Yes, you may be older, but you're also wiser. Find a new and innovative way to make your dreams come true. It's never too late to begin again.

**Take a Do-Over**

Do you remember playing games as a kid? And if you lost, screaming: "DO OVER!!!" Some of us need a Do-Over. If you're not happy with the choices and decisions you've made that have led to this point in your life, maybe it's time for a Do-Over. There is no reason why we can't call a Do-Over as adults. Just the thought of a Do-Over means everything is erased and you get to start over with an entirely clean slate. Are you happy with your life? Are you pleased with your decisions? Are you at peace with the people closest to you? If not, then, maybe it's time for a Do-Over. Remember, it's never too late to begin again.

You need to follow your dreams and goals and not try to fulfill the beliefs and expectations of everyone else around you. Are you living the life you envisioned for yourself? Are you where you thought you would be by now? Or are you living someone else's dreams; like your parent's or partner's, or maybe even society's dream of what they say you should be?

No matter what your past has been, your future can be anything you choose. Life allows for U-turns and Do-Overs, so take one if you need it. You can pick any point in time to take do a Do-Over. That's the best thing about a Do-Over, nothing before the Do-Over counts.

## Goals Are Golden

*"Your goals must be crystal clear so your brain understands them."*

It has been said that only 3 percent of people have clearly defined life goals in writing; and consequently, those 3 percent are the most successful people.

One of the great ironies of life is that you don't have to be a genius to be a success. Please don't misunderstand. The point is not that we should strive for mediocrity or inferior performance based on our abilities, but even an idiot can be successful if he has written goals, a blueprint, and the will to succeed. A lot of smart and talented people waste a lot of time doing nothing and going nowhere because they're running around in circles, expending precious energy and resources with no results.

Think about this: A genius can be running around in circles and never get anywhere if he doesn't have a plan. If you gave an idiot a map—or even better, a GPS with voice-activated directions—even he (or she) would figure out how to get where he is going. But if the genius doesn't have a map or some other guide, he will never know where to start or where he is going, ultimately achieving nothing. There are a lot of really smart and talented people who have nothing to show for it, because they didn't have a plan for success.

Some people are doing better than others in life not because they are more intelligent or more educated, but because they do things differently. It is not because they are better. The reason they're getting better results is because they are doing things with purpose, on purpose. Simply put, they have a plan.

In order to write this book I wrote an outline so I didn't forget what I wanted to say, and so I could organize what I wanted to share. I want you to do the same thing. Outline your dreams. Outline your future.

Make a blueprint for your life. Make a plan. Work your plan. Follow your plan. Don't give up. Plans work!

Sometimes I think the idea of goal-setting or defining goals can be scary or overwhelming to some people, so they become paralyzed by fear and don't do anything at all. That's why I prefer using the terms "blueprint" or "life strategy" – because they sound less intimidating and threatening. Using those terms sounds more like a declaration that things are going to happen no matter what, rather than using the term "goals," which sounds like something you could potentially miss, and then perceive it to be a failure.

Whether you think of your life plan as a blueprint, outline, or a map, it's evident that people set goals for a reason – because we need a way to measure what we have or have not accomplished. A race without a finish line is just a bunch of people out running. A soccer field without soccer goals to measure and keep score produces a couple of teams running and kicking a ball around in circles for no reason. A business without a plan is just an idea whose time hasn't yet come. Simply put, goal-setting is your blueprint for success - it is how to take where you are and get to where you want to go.

It's a good way to keep score and a great way to measure your progress.

Setting goals isn't required just to keep from failing; it's also to keep from succeeding too quickly in a way that is unmanageable. Successful leaders understand the concepts of "managed growth," "smart growth," and "sustainable growth." Those are ways to plan for success, control success, and keep success. To create your ideal life or anything else, you must have a strong foundation to support its development. If you do not have a strong foundation, the structure will strain under the pressure of what is built on top, and then collapse. When I owned my RE/MAX offices, they became so successful so fast that the situation was destined to implode around me, rendering me and my staff helpless to support the rate of growth. The basic business infrastructure was there, but I didn't have enough systems in place to support additional growth because I didn't expect it to grow as fast as it did. Maintaining that level of success became very difficult. Instead of building and layering more opportunities on a solid foundation, it felt more like overloading a small foundation with a huge weight, making the entire enterprise shaky and unstable. Your life's blueprint should anticipate all levels of growth, so that you have a plan in place to manage it.

As part of the planning process, be ready for what success will cost you. Attaining your goals and dreams comes at a cost, whether it is time, money, relationships, etc. Decide now if you are willing and able to pay the cost and weather the storm – and decide now whether it is worth it in the long run.

## You Need to Have a Target

*"Most people aim for nothing and hit it with amazing accuracy."*

It's time to get going and do something! Great American author and lecturer Ralph Waldo Emerson quoted, "Without ambition, one starts nothing. Without work, one finishes nothing." Over the years of working as an electrician and real estate broker, getting married and divorced, raising children as a single mom and becoming an entrepreneur and author, I've learned that life is not about getting a chance, it's about taking a chance. Once you identify the chance you plan to take, then comes time for the blueprint to chart the path, where it should lead, and how long that particular journey should take.

Consider how significant it is to chart a course for international travel. One small change or shift in direction mid-flight, can take an airplane completely off course. For example, if a plane is flying from California to Hawaii and is just a little bit off course when it leaves California—by the time it gets to Hawaii (a small series of islands)—each missed checkpoint and every unintended shift will result in the plane being lost out in the middle of the ocean, with no islands in sight and nowhere to land. Our lives can be a lot like that when we don't have a plan and written strategy to keep us on track. That explains how and why so many people slowly drift away from their dreams. Suddenly, one day they realize that they aren't where they wanted to be. "Dream Drift" doesn't happen suddenly or overnight; it happens slowly, steadily, and systematically while we're asleep at the wheel and inundated with the daily tasks of day-to-day living. Wake up!

Don't forget to adjust your course each and every day as you follow your dreams in order to keep your life headed in the right direction. For that reason, it is important to not only write a blueprint for your goals, but to measure and monitor them also. That process keeps you on track and gets you to your destination. It's OK to continually adjust your course as needed, due to emergencies, opportunities, and unforeseen circumstances. However, it's not OK to wing it. Create a plan, follow the plan, monitor the plan, adjust the plan, embrace the plan, and complete the plan.

As with any plan, you should begin with the end in mind. Always work your blueprint backwards. This is known as the Merlin Principle, because the wizard Merlin lived his life backwards.

Decide what it is you want to do and by when. Then work your way backwards. Figure out what you must do to achieve your final goal. Then figure out what you have to do to accomplish the steps to get to your final goal. Continue working backwards until you have an actual plan, outline, and starting point. You must have due dates, which you can adjust if necessary, but put in place a deadline to accomplish your goals and then get busy. A goal is simply a dream with a deadline.

## Declare It As True

*"Declare it, See it, Track it, Achieve it."* ~Donna Palm

Declare it as if it was true. Always state your plans, blueprints, or goals in a positive light. In other words, move toward your goal not away from it. Always state your dreams and goals as if they have already happened. For example, if you want to lose weight, do not state your goal as 'I want to lose 20 pounds.' State your goal as, 'I am my ideal weight of 150 pounds.' Always state your goal as 'I am' rather than 'I want to be.' It is an exercise in creating reality in your mind. You don't need to create the idea of wanting something because it will reinforce the idea of simply "wanting it" forever. Your mind's reality should be that you have it, not that you want it. If you state it in a positive way, as in 'I am,' it establishes a point of achievement and a point of success. If you say I want to be a millionaire, you will always want to be a millionaire. The idea is to get your mind to believe it as true. If you say, I am a millionaire by a certain date, and follow through with your plans to achieve it, your mind is more likely to believe it as a truth, and then subconsciously align everything toward that truth and create the positive environment to achieve that truth.

## Who Do You Need To Be?

When what you pursue eludes you, it's like chasing cats. Instead, discover who you need to be in order to achieve what you want. Instead of chasing something, let it come to you by being what it takes to achieve your successes. For example: being accountable, being your word, being positive, being healthy, being time-efficient, being disciplined, being logical, being spiritual, being committed, being invincible, being persistent, being tenacious, being thirsty for knowledge, etc., all align with being who you want to be. Remember to avoid behaviors that don't align with who you want to be because success is not what you do, it's who you are.

Make a list outlining the characteristics of who you need to be from the inside-out in order to complete what you want to achieve. Start thinking about how to become who you need to be. You will be surprised by the results. This is a very refreshing exercise to do. It opens up your eyes to what you are capable of and what is possible. It can be very inspiring.

Ask yourself these questions and take notes so you can look back on them:

1. Who do I have to be in order to attract what and who I want into my life?

2. Who do I have to be in order achieve what I want to achieve?

Your personal self-image can make or break you. All your successes and accomplishments, as well as your failures and disappointments, start from the inside.

3. What does my inner "self-talk" consist of?

This could be equaled to your inner strength or inner power. Harnessing your inner strength is extremely important when it comes to success.

4. What are my habits; both good habits and bad habits?

5. Are there any habits I need to change?

Don't beat yourself up or be judgmental, but understand that the habits you have will help you succeed or hold you back. Go through different areas of your life and see how these habits affect different areas of your life both in positive and negative ways. Think about what is limiting you or preventing you from raising your standards and pushing yourself a little harder.

**What's Your Why?**

You must have a very strong WHY if you're going to reach the pinnacle of success. If you don't have a reason to do something, you're not going to do it. I call it Why Power.

Having a strong Why actually makes the hard, grueling, or even boring aspects of your plan much easier. Heck, many times you don't even see things as obstacles when you want something bad enough and when your Why is strong enough.

Sometimes staying motivated can be extremely difficult. Anybody can be excited at the beginning. But as time goes by, the excitement wears off and things start to get more difficult... that's when the true test begins. This is when you have to go back to your Why; and if your Why is not strong enough, you won't succeed. If your Why isn't strong enough, you need to change the reason why you're pursuing a goal and redefine your purpose to have more meaning. Your Why Power should be strong enough to fuel your dream all the way to completion.

Example: There's a difference between willpower and Why Power. It is one thing to have enough willpower to not eat peanuts because you're trying to save on calories. It's another thing to not eat peanuts because you have a severe nut allergy, in which eating the peanuts could kill you. Tell me which example is a stronger "why" not to eat the peanuts.

During accidents, people have been known to lift cars off the ground to save someone pinned underneath. This super-human strength can be attributed to a very strong Why. Hopefully, you will never need to go to this extreme. But when times are tough, your Why might be all you have to keep you going and inspire you to succeed.

An example of my Why when I was an industrial electrician was, "if I quit, they win." It became my mantra at the time. I would say it to myself over and over again. Back then, I was the only woman on most construction sites with hundreds of men. Many times I was sexually harassed, ridiculed, or demeaned for being there. Any time I did anything, I had to be 10 times better than the guys just to be acknowledged. Many times even if I accomplished something, I would not get credit for it and I would have to prove myself time and time again. No matter how hard it was both physically and mentally, because it was a very grueling job in both ways, I would never allow myself to quit. Because "if I quit, they win," and I simply was not about to let them win. Over the years I became more and more successful in the industry. Often I was doing a much better job than men with many more years of experience than I had. That made many of them very upset, especially when they were passed over for opportunities that were offered to me. Many of them said I only got the job because I was a woman, so that made me fight even harder not to quit when times got tough. Eventually I ended up in supervision and was actually the boss of several of these men. My Why is what kept me going through the difficult times and gave me the ability to succeed in a challenging industry. Don't ever underestimate the power of a strong Why. What's Your Why?

## Let's Start Blueprinting

*"We get out of life what we dream, create, and put into life."*
~Donna Palm

One of the best ways to start Blueprinting is with a review.

Make several lists that you can review and keep in front of you, so they are clear in your mind. Yes, this is your homework, so get out the notebook or use the ledger in the back of this book. No complaining… make it fun!

Summary Blueprint - Describe your ideal life:

_____
_____
_____
_____
_____
_____
_____

*Dream Bigger, Live Better*

_____
_____
_____

GRATITUDE LIST: Make a list of everything you are grateful for. Include all areas of your life, including family, friends, talents you have, things you have, opportunities that are available to you, etc. Think long and hard, and leave no stone unturned. This is the gratitude list you will be going back to when times get tough and you need some inspiration. If you have a happy or inspiring story from your past, include it on your list. Remember this is to be a positive and inspiring exercise.

_____
_____
_____
_____
_____
_____
_____
_____

ACCOMPLISHMENTS LIST: Make a list of your greatest accomplishments so far in life. No matter how small they may seem, write them down. You may need the inspiration when times get tough and you are feeling like a failure. You will need written proof when you are in a negative mindset that you are not a failure and you are loaded with self-worth.

_____
_____
_____
_____
_____
_____
_____
_____

SCHOOL OF LIFE LIST: Make a list of the greatest lessons you have learned so far in life. This is your school of life list. What have you learned from life? What have you learned never to do again? What are some successful patterns that should be repeated as habits? There is a reason we learn in life. Don't forget the lessons learned, or you will be doomed to repeat them until you do learn.

_____
_____
_____
_____
_____
_____
_____

SELF-IMPROVEMENT LIST: Make a list of personal improvements that you have made from your life lessons. This will inspire you during times when you are frustrated because you repeated the same mistakes; yes, it happens to all of us. When you feel dumb because you made the same mistake more than once, refer to this list of self-improvements to prove to yourself you have learned from your past mistakes. Sometimes it takes more than once to get it right.

_____
_____

_____

_____

_____

_____

_____

_____

SMARTEST DECISIONS LIST: Make a list of the smartest decisions you have ever made. If it ain't broke, don't fix it, right? Think about all the times you really hit the ball out of the park. How did you approach the information and what process did you use to make a final decision? Make a note of what works for you and then repeat it when necessary. This list also will encourage you on days when you feel like you can't do anything right.

_____

_____

_____

_____

_____

*Dream Bigger, Live Better*

_____
_____
_____

DO SOMETHING DIFFERENT LIST: Make a list of things you would do differently. It's said that hindsight is 20/20. Looking back, what different choices would you make that could have changed the outcome or course of your life? This is another life lesson to consider so that you don't repeat the same mistakes over and over again.

_____
_____
_____
_____
_____
_____
_____

LUCKY LIST: Make a list of the "Luck" you have had in your life. We know luck prevails when preparation meets opportunity, however sometimes you just need a little "Luck" to give you an unexpected break or that surge of eclectic joy in life and the boost you need to keep going.

_____

_____

_____

_____

_____

_____

_____

Keep these Blueprint Lists in a handy place where you can find them at a moment's notice. The lists will help keep you on track when you're tempted to venture off the path. Plus, you'll be surprised how far a little reminder or inspiration can go when you need it.

While the Blueprint maps out how to get to your destination, the actual Life Plan tells you (and others) where you're going. If we really want to enjoy life and be successful, we need balance. So let's make a plan that balances all the significant areas of our lives.

## Life Plan

How would you like to be remembered? Now is the time to start building the legacy of your life. Don't think of your legacy in terms of how people will remember you when you're gone; but instead, think of it in terms of how will you impact others while you live, work, play, travel, connect, influence, and socialize now.

In order to help create life balance and happiness, distinguish what your life plan is rather than just your business plan. In other words, what kind of life do you want to live? What quality of life do you want? Where do you want to live? How do you want to live? What do you want to do every day? How many hours a day do you want to work? How will you spend your free time? Do you want to be home at a certain time for dinner every day? Do you want to have time for your kid's soccer games? Do you want to travel or work close to home? How do you want to dress? Do you want to wear business clothes or casual clothes all day long; work outside or inside; travel a little or a lot? When you make your future life plan, be sure to begin with the end in mind.

Most of us plan our lives incorrectly. We think only about the success of work and making money, and forget about the rest of our lives. It's easy to forget that if we're working all the time, even if we have plenty of money, we won't necessarily be able to enjoy other areas of our lives.

What decisions or changes do you need to make to have the life you desire? With every choice there are consequences; sometimes good, sometimes bad, and sometimes ugly. Regardless, life is a never-ending series of decisions that create situations we have to face and address. So, make up your mind now about what's really important and make those choices that create the life you want – and the type of life you want to be remembered by.

Reflect on all the areas of your life – spiritual, family, financial, work, business, free time, health, etc. Think of how you would like them to be and picture yourself in those various settings. Outline the elements of each area and write them down. This is the beginning of your new life plan.

*Spiritual*

Too many people ignore the spiritual aspect of their lives, when in fact, spirituality is the foundation. Don't make the mistake of confusing religion with spirituality, because they are different. While religion is generally based on tradition, doctrine, repetition, and rituals, spirituality is an acknowledgement that you are a small part of something greater that is divinely connected to your life and its purpose. It is the belief system that is the centering point of your life. So, what would you like your spiritual life to look like one year from now? What would inspire you to fulfill your potential? How can you obtain inner peace? How can you connect with your external and internal sources of energy? Make a list of ideas. Does it include practicing your faith, volunteering, giving back to your community, meditating for clarity, or sharing with others? Do one, some, or all of those things to strengthen your spiritual life and also to build the strong foundation for the rest of your life.

*Relational*

Probably the second most important area in your life is your relationships. These include relationships with family, friends, co-workers, and basically anyone you are in contact with. What would you like this area of your life to look like one year from now? Are you in healthy relationships with the people closest to you; those in your inner circle? If so, how can you show appreciation to them or even improve the relationships? Are you in any unhealthy relationships? Do any relationships take away your energy, self-respect, or self-worth? As you reflect on the relationships in your life, make a determination on whether it's possible to improve the relationship or better to simply cut the ties and move on. Remember you cannot rescue someone else – they need to rescue themselves. Sometimes you need to move on and love people from a distance while they work on improving their own lives and constructing their own life plans. Make an effort to be in relationships that energize and inspire you. Cultivate relationships with positive, like-minded people who will raise your energy, self-worth, and inspire you to be better.

*Mental*

Never stop growing. The mental aspect of your life is all about your inner growth; how you see the world, yourself, and your ability to thrive where you are. The Bible tells us that as we think, so we become. What are you thinking about? Be careful, because your thoughts lead to actions; your actions lead to habits; and your habits define your future. What type of information and entertainment are you allowing to occupy space in your mind? Remember the statement: "garbage in, garbage out?" Well, that's as true for computers and technology as it is for our bodies and minds. What would you like to learn? What new skill, talent, or ability should you fine-tune to improve your overall success rate in life? Make a list of topics, workshops, seminars, or books to learn from this year. Consider learning a new language too; not just French, Spanish, or Mandarin, but how about learning the languages of social media, sports, technology, or anything that's outside of your normal comfort zone. Learning means growing, so don't be afraid to venture outside of the world you know – into an arena that may open your eyes to a whole new world of possibilities.

*Physical*

A famous comedian once said, "I know that beauty is only skin deep, but ugly goes straight to the bone." How's that for social commentary on the importance of physical beauty? While it's true that the "real you" is on the inside, we cannot neglect the fact and importance that other people still see you from the outside-in, not the other way around. Here's what I believe- make no apologies for being smart and beautiful – outside and inside. There is absolutely nothing wrong with maximizing your physical beauty so that you can feel good about yourself and confident in how you present yourself. The danger is allowing other people, publications, and peer pressure to define you based solely on your physical characteristics. Make a life plan for your physical appearance, just as you would anything else. How would you like to be physically in the next year? Are you at your ideal weight? Do you take proper care of your health? Are you mindful of what you put into your body? You can have all of the money in the world, but if you don't have your health, then you don't have anything. And if you don't love and feel good about yourself, it's nearly impossible to feel good about anything else.

*Business*

You don't have to own a business to be in business. Running your life, managing a household, directing charitable non-profit work can all have the same challenges as a structured for-profit business. Each year, companies undertake a review of their business plan, business projections, and conduct a S.W.O.T. Analysis that identifies their Strengths, Weaknesses, Opportunities, and Threats. What would a S.W.O.T. Analysis of your life look like? What strengths do you have that you can use to propel you where you want to go? What challenges or weaknesses are possibly holding you back and preventing you from pursuing or achieving your goals? What opportunities are on the horizon or right in front of you that you can take advantage of to advance to the next level in your life? What is threatening your success; is it fear, anxiety, or just not knowing what the future holds? You'll find that a

"S.W.O.T." Analysis is an easy and efficient way to assess your life and then make plans to adapt or adjust as needed. Once that information has been identified, take strides toward finding the answers you need to get the results you want. Do you need to find a mentor to help direct you? Do you need a specific kind of training or education? Do you need financial backing or professional support? Make a list of your long-term desires and break down what—and who—you will need to accomplish them.

### My S.W.O.T. Analysis

Strengths (internal)

_____

_____

_____

_____

_____

Weaknesses/Challenges (internal)

_____

_____

_____

_____

_____

Opportunities (external)

_____

_____

_____

_____

_____

Threats (external source)

_____

_____

_____

_____

_____

*Financial*

Our society tends to blame money (or the lack thereof) for a lot of things. But, over the years I've learned that money isn't good, it isn't bad, it just is. All different types of people have money, and they use it for different purposes—some good and some bad. Even if money isn't the hero or villain we sometimes make it out to be, there is a distinct advantage to knowing your true financial status and assessing your financial health. When it comes to the financial portion of your life, think long-term as well as short-term. Don't get overwhelmed, but instead approach your financial health in small, manageable steps. How much money do you have in the bank? How about in investments or retirement plans? How much do you make, owe, and spend? Be sure to include all debts, credit cards, car loans, home loans, student loans, savings, investments, retirement accounts, etc. Don't be in denial. Based on what you can afford, enlist the support of a financial planner, financial adviser, financial specialist, or a good spreadsheet to help you get organized and get started in developing your financial life plan. Tackling this challenge head-on is the only way to conquer whatever financial issues you have. What small changes can you make toward improving your financial situation within the next year? Every little step counts, and help is available if you need it. The sooner you organize your finances, the sooner you can move forward. The inner peace you will feel once you are financially organized and on the path to financial stability and financial independence is worth the time and energy spent.

*Lifestyle*

Like I said before; Life is short, so you have to get it all in while you can. Start designing your dreams now. Your lifestyle list should be fun to think about and fun to make, so don't leave anything out. This is the list you refer to when you have had a long hard day and ask yourself, 'Why am I working so hard?' Let your mind run wild, since these are the joys of life – the things that make life worth living. This is how you will live your everyday life and the experiences that will shape who you are and what you become. Don't wait - plan it now because time is wasting. On your lifestyle list, include travel, hobbies, where you want to live, and what type of car you'd like to drive. Don't forget about adventures, fine dining, and people you would like to meet. Would you like to dance, sing, or play an instrument? Would you like to see the world, experience new cultures, do something thrilling, altruistic, or amazing? Plans must be made in order to squeeze everything in, so get started now because your life is waiting for you to live it!

Now that we have covered the seven main areas of life, revisit your plans and make a list of the Top 10 things you would like to accomplish in the next year. Go through and make sub-lists or a plan under each one explaining what it will take to get these things done. Set deadlines for each item. These deadlines can be flexible, but the idea is to have a deadline so there are pressure points, benchmarks, and a finish line. Remember, goals without deadlines are just dreams. Plus, deadlines create accountability and help put some structure to the plan. Be very clear in defining what is considered as completion of a task – and no cheating allowed.

After you have completed the list of goals as well as your plans regarding what it will take to achieve them, go over your list one more time. Which Top 3 goals really jump out at you? Or here's another way to think about it. Which Top 3 goals—when you accomplish them—will make the most difference in your life? They might be the hardest ones to achieve or the easiest; it doesn't matter. Pick the top three that mean the most to you. These are going to be your POWER GOALS.

*Dream Bigger, Live Better*

Select these top three POWER GOALS from the list and start on them immediately. No excuses, no procrastination, get started now! This is the blueprint for your Life Plan; now let's start building the life you've planned.

## CHAPTER 2

### WHAT ARE YOU WAITING FOR?

*"Get in the game. Don't sit on the sidelines and waste your life."*

~Donna Palm

Interestingly enough, most people are waiting for something every single day. Statisticians suggest that most people spend 45 to 62 minutes waiting each and every day. Over the course of a 70-year adult lifespan, that means individuals spend approximately 3 years of their lives waiting... at traffic signals, in bank lines, at gas pumps, in movie theaters, in airports, in grocery store check-out lines, or waiting for technology downloads and other conveniences that are meant to make the mundane tasks of life more efficient. What are you waiting for?

If you sit back and wait for perfect timing and perfect conditions before you get started, nothing will ever get done. I agree with the saying that, "a good plan today is better than a perfect plan tomorrow." Why? Because we don't have any idea what tomorrow holds—or if tomorrow is even coming—but what we do have is today. It's time to stop waiting and get going.

My belief is that life is too short to spend it waiting to go after what you want. When I'm nervous, anxious, or hesitant to get started on a goal, the first thing I do is set myself up to win. I create a fail-proof, fool-proof goal to boost my self-esteem and my level of confidence. Sometimes, all you need is a win! If you need to jumpstart your adrenaline to get things moving, give yourself a ridiculously easy goal—something that's significant and important—but not complicated or time-consuming. The idea is to gather momentum through the art of completion, which ultimately builds confidence.

### The Enemy of Inertia

What are you waiting for, and Why are you waiting? Many of us are battling the enemy of inertia. Remember the law of inertia from middle and high school? It states that a body at rest will remain at rest, and a body in motion will maintain that same path of motion in a straight line, unless acted upon by an external force. In other words, when we are sitting idly on our dreams, there is a great likelihood that we will remain idle. And if we've fallen victim to complacency—stuck in a dead-end job, with no opportunities for advancement or no way out—we tend to stay stuck and miserable until an external influence (like money, bills, depression, or termination) forces our hand and twists our arms into doing something different. Although a swift kick in the behind every now and then can be a good thing, that should be the exception, not the norm.

There's no reason and no excuse not to get going. It doesn't matter how much time has already passed, it's never too late to start pursuing your passion. Saying that you're too busy, too tired, too young, or too old won't work any longer.

Grandma Moses was a famous American folk artist. She didn't start painting until well into her 70s. As her paintings of rural America became more iconic, so did her level of fame. While in her 80s and 90s (during the 1950s), her art exhibitions broke attendance records all over the world. In 1960, in honor of her 100th birthday, Grandma Moses was featured on the cover of Life Magazine. I believe that anyone who achieves success in life has some sort of turning point. At some point in time, they all of a sudden make a decision to change and go after their dreams. After that, their life is never the same again. It can happen at any age. It can happen in your 20s or it can happen in your 70s (like it did for Grandma Moses). Your spark of genius or ingenuity doesn't have an expiration date, but it won't happen by itself. You have to get going.

There is an amazing woman named Shirley Minter-Smith who lives by the philosophy that "What You Want, Wants You." Here's why I think she is so amazing: Shirley battled obesity and the death of her son from brain cancer, but simply chose not to give up. Sure, she could have given in to depression, thrown in the towel, and decided that life was no longer worth the trouble. But Shirley took a different approach. She decided to turn her pain into passion and inspire others to live to their fullest potential. Shirley made a new blueprint plan for her future – to pursue the life she wanted to live. It started with becoming healthier. She changed her mind. She changed her habits, and as a result, she changed her life.

Shirley is an amazing testament to the power of the human spirit. She lost more than 100 pounds—half her body weight—and decided to become a professional bodybuilder at age 60. That's not a typo, age 6-0. Not only that, she began competing and won two national bodybuilding championships - and then was awarded the Iron Female Athlete of the Year. On her email, voicemail, and in person, the first thing she shares is that "What You Want, Wants You," a reminder for all of us to never give up on our dreams. The point is that if Shirley can accomplish all of that at age 60, then What Are You Waiting For, and Why Are You Still Waiting?

**The Someday Syndrome**

Many of us are still fighting battles from our past, which are holding us hostage and keeping us from our dreams. We remember past failures. We remember past discouragement and disappointments, and then we decide that we're still the same person who failed before. Instead of learning from those lessons, we get stuck and stagnate. That's where many people catch what I call the "Someday Syndrome." Does any of this sound familiar?

'Someday I will go back to school. Someday I will start a business of my own. Someday I will travel and see the world. Someday I will pursue my passion.' When is "someday" finally going to arrive? For most people, "someday" never comes, and as a result, a lot of dreams die. Don't live in a "someday world" and don't say I'll do it "someday"; whatever it is, do it now. Another word for "someday" is procrastination, and it's usually based on fear. Unfortunately, "someday" is usually "no day," and that's the real tragedy and disappointment that we should all fear.

If you tend to fall victim to the Someday Syndrome because your dreams and goals seem too big to tackle, then change your approach. You don't have to do everything all at once. Take small bites to get the big success. Divide goals into manageable pieces so that you don't get overwhelmed, and so you feel successful along the way. During a college freshman orientation session, the dean of students asked a simple, but intriguing question. She said, "How do you eat an elephant?" The students looked around, not sure what to think or how to respond. Again, the dean asked, "How do you eat an elephant?" She waited, but there was still no response from the students. Then she answered her own question: "One bite at a time." The point was that their new journey to obtain a college education probably seemed large and insurmountable on Day 1; the equivalent of eating an elephant. However, if they simply took one day at a time, each step as it came, one challenge after another; when all was said and done, they would have "eaten" the elephant and accomplished their goals. So now, I'm asking you… "How do you eat an elephant?" The answer hasn't changed: One bite at a time.

## On Your Mark...

Some people quit before they even get started. They dream a dream, aspire to accomplish something great, but focus on all the obstacles, challenges, and reasons for failure, and then talk themselves out of moving forward. Have you ever quit before you really got started on something you desired to do? Or have you started a project or goal, and then run out of steam or momentum because you got tired or became discouraged? If so, you're definitely not alone. The world is full of partial projects, unfinished books, incomplete ideas, and undiscovered inventions from people who started, but didn't finish. Unfortunately, the result of leaving a dream unfulfilled is usually regret.

Look back over the events of your life. If you are like most people, the biggest regrets you have are the chances you never took; not the chances you took and failed. If you never take a chance, you automatically fail. If you do take a chance, there's a possibility that you still might fail, but at least you'll be "failing forward," which is the pathway that leads to success.

I recently witnessed a perfect example of this from my own life. As I was wrapping up the final chapters in this book, I had a life-changing experience. So much so, I felt I had to come back and add it to this section. For me, it was a perfect example of regretting that I didn't take a chance.

A very good friend of mine owns several RE/MAX offices in the Midwest. For the last few years, he has been traveling across the country on his Harley-Davidson motorcycle in the summertime. It is a beautiful bike designed for cross-country travel. This past spring he asked me to go on a couple of cross-country rides with him. At that time, I had never even been on a motorcycle. I live in Florida and in my area we have a very high rate of accidents due to tourists not knowing the area and several other factors, so I have always been terrified of getting on a motorcycle. I really wanted to go with him, but I would not let myself get past my fear. I started making plans with him, but at the last minute "my schedule" would always get in the way. While it was true I did have a few scheduling conflicts, to be honest, I was really grateful when I did so I had an excuse not to get past my fear. I could tell he was becoming increasingly disappointed with my last-minute cancellations and rejections. Deep down, I felt awful. Now, my fear was affecting his happiness as well as mine.

Finally, in August we met in Canada at the RE/MAX owners meetings. I flew up from Florida and he rode his Harley to Ottawa. I had finally agreed to go on a ride across New England with him. On the last day of the meetings we shipped our business suits home, put on the leather and the helmets, and pulled out of the 5-star hotel on his Harley.

I never thought I would last more than a day. I thought he would have to drop me off at the nearest airport to catch a flight home. What happened next was indescribable. Let's just say... now I understand the Harley Fever.

It was AMAZING!!!!! Riding the bike was a completely different experience than riding in the car. I could see with a clarity I had never seen before. I could smell every freshly-mown blade of grass, every flower blooming, and the crisp mist of every waterfall we passed. The views were incredible; from the majestic green mountains, the clear blue ocean, the towering cities, the rolling farms, the rich coal mines, to the grazing farm animals and the wild animals including deer, moose, and cougars. From the quaint country inns of Vermont, to enjoying freshly caught lobsters on the coast of Maine and seeing our nation's Capital, I felt so inspired, so American, seeing the diversity of our country from the back of a motorcycle. In five and a half days we traveled 2,400 miles through 17 states, plus Canada and Washington, DC, usually riding 10-11 hours a day. The days seemed to fly by. It was one of the most incredible experiences of my life. So much so, I have since learned how to ride, earned my license and can't wait to ride again.

So what is the moral of the story? Yes, it is obvious. I now have a huge regret. Because I was not willing to face my fears, not only did I hurt someone else's feelings, but I missed out on the incredible experiences I could have had on the previous rides. For the rest of my life I am going to regret not taking a chance sooner. I am grateful, however, that I did face my fear or I never would be where I am now, able to ride and enjoy the exhilaration of riding a Harley. What a valuable lesson I learned. When you think about facing your fears, think of what I missed and what you could be missing too.

Here's the greater lesson: Don't look back over your decisions and your life with a sense of regret because regret is more painful and more disappointing than failure. Don't go through life living 'what if' or I could have or I wish I had. Light a fire under yourself; the time to start is now. Momentum is everything. Create momentum moving toward the things you desire and you can get there faster and more efficiently. Don't wait for perfect conditions, just go and get started. There is never going to be a perfect time. Don't wait. Don't forget that if anything goes wrong, you can always take a "Do-Over." That's what Do-Overs, U-turns, and workarounds are for. Perfect the process as you go forward and learn. Even if it's scary, face the fear, harness the adrenaline, and run with it!

*"Risking failure is the only chance you have in life to succeed."*
~Donna Palm

### Get Motivated to Get Going…

We get out of life what we dream, create, and put into life. Nothing worth having is not worth the work getting there. Think about it. The odds of winning the lottery are one in several million. The odds of you achieving your goals and dreams are much better than that, so don't waste your time sitting around waiting to win the lottery – odds are that it will never happen. However, if you get your buns in gear and pursue your hopes, dreams, and goals, you are sure to get there much more quickly and more efficiently than waiting to win the lottery.

All successful people and great leaders have the motivation to succeed. They are not necessarily smarter, more educated, or more intelligent than others, but the thing they all have in common is the drive to succeed that pushes them forward through difficult times. They are motivated, persistent, and tenacious. These people take action while others sit on the sidelines and watch. They do not wait for things to come to them, instead, they go out and get them. Success also requires surrounding yourself with other high-energy, positive, and motivated people. Like the saying goes, you play better golf with better golfers.

Without question, it is easier to be motivated when you are building up momentum and speed and your dreams are progressing nicely. It is the true test of a driven person to be able to motivate themselves and keep moving forward in times of crisis and challenges. In my own life, I've found that it is best to look at the challenges in a positive light; as an external force that squashes the enemy of inertia and that can propel you closer to your dreams.

I've also learned that everyone can be motivated, but everyone is motivated differently. For example, just about anyone who sticks their hand into fire is motivated to pull it out – because the pain and consequences are too great to withstand. But not everyone is motivated by money or financial success, because that reward may not be fulfilling enough. Some people are motivated by internal rewards like the feeling of satisfaction that comes from helping others.

Some people are driven by production or by tangible, measurable achievement. Some people are driven by relationships and they may be the types who are motivated by approval or being liked by others. Some people like stability and are driven to maintain the status quo; they like predictability and consistency. Some people love change and variety and are motivated by new adventures and new experiences.

Oftentimes people who like stability may get stuck due to their fear of change. They may be slow to take action and miss opportunities because they experience Analysis Paralysis or are resistant to change and innovation.

On the other hand, people who love change sometimes jump in too quickly. They may get so excited about a new idea or opportunity that they don't research or plan properly and may act without thinking things through.

People who are driven by relationships can often be people pleasers, which can be good; however, they may lose themselves and who they are and who they want to be because they are so busy pleasing others. They also may be the type of people who need to make a positive difference in the world and value making contributions to the world. They enjoy doing meaningful work and feel good about what they are doing. Personal compliments are usually huge rewards to them.

People who are driven by tangible assets may lose out in the relationship department sometimes. People who are driven by outside sources enjoy public recognition and financial compensation. This does not mean they cannot be generous people, it just means that compensation is often a major motivator.

Motivation creates action. You must determine what motivates you as an individual. Many people don't even know what motivates them, so it's important to spend a little time discovering what motivates you. This goes back to the Why. Why are you driven, and why do you want the things you want? If your Why is not strong enough, you will not be driven or have the necessary momentum to keep going when it matters most. Your quality of life and the ability to live your dreams are dependent on your motivation.

## Getting Lazy After Success

When you are under pressure you have an adrenaline rush. Having your back up against the wall gives you a stronger drive for success and a strong reason to get things done. As a result, you can accomplish so much more.

After achieving a goal, it can be your riskiest time to drift. You lose your adrenaline once you achieve your goals and may have a tendency to slack off. This has happened to me many times, including after I sold my two RE/MAX offices.

When I first moved to Florida and started my own company, I was doing so much more because the pressure was on. Everyone would ask me how in the world I could run two RE/MAX offices; handle all my customers that I sold real estate to, handle raising two children all by myself, handle maintaining the house and everything else. I was riding the adrenaline wave of success.

My main office was the most successful real estate office in the area at the time. After I sold my real estate offices, I lost my adrenaline rush. I noticed for several years after I sold my offices that my back was no longer up against the wall. I thought I would enjoy the semi-retirement by spending more time with my children. Instead I slacked off and got lazy. Even though I was still very successful with real estate sales, even in the worst downturn in the history of the market, I did not give it my all. I know I could have achieved much more if I had put forth the effort. My heart was just not in it. For several years, I barely succeeded at anything I tried to accomplish just because I lost my Why. I lost my adrenaline rush and my heart wasn't in it.

As time went on, I started new projects and had new opportunities. The adrenaline was starting to flow again and I was finding what I tried suddenly was more successful again. I was back in the game.

After achieving a goal, especially if it is a large one, pay attention to your mindset. It is best to get back on the horse right away and go after the next goal so you don't end up resting on your laurels for too long.

**Getting Re-motivated**

No one is driven or motivated 100 percent of the time. There were many times in my life when I was down and had to struggle to get back in the game. For example, years ago I lived in my car because I had nowhere else to live. More recently, I had a business partner who deceived me, betrayed my trust, and emotionally and financially hurt me. I have been through divorces, abusive relationships, and financial challenges just to name a few things. But I know I'm not the only one; you've probably been through tough times too.

A successful and driven person can get tossed in the rodeo of life just like anyone else. The difference is how quickly they brush themselves off and get back up on the horse again. Do you think Oprah Winfrey—arguably one of the most successful women in the world—never has a day where things don't go as well as she would like? During an interview in 2013, she admitted to nearly experiencing a nervous breakdown. Early on, one of her pet movie projects failed and then years later her TV network initially struggled to gain its footing. Do you honestly think she didn't feel any emotional pain and rejection? She is one of the most successful women in the world, but yet she feels pain and rejection just like everyone else. Still, she is strong, inspired, and driven. She started from humble beginnings, overcame seemingly insurmountable obstacles, and achieved amazing success all while helping others along the way.

There will be times when you get discouraged and feel like giving up too; don't think it won't happen to you, because it happens to everyone. There will be failures and there will be embarrassments. That's just part of life. These are learning experiences to make you stronger. Never listen to the naysayers. Failure for them is ammunition. It gives them a chance to say they told you so. Prove them wrong and don't quit. In doing this, you may also inspire them. Maybe they will be willing to take a chance. And even if they fail, they may be willing to get back up and try again.

## Competition

How do you handle being under pressure due to competition? In many situations if you're facing competition it already means you are one of the best in whatever you are doing in the first place.

My daughter was chosen to play cello for the high school-level Florida State Orchestra. She was extremely nervous about auditioning for her seating position in the orchestra. My advice to her was: first of all, relax and enjoy it. Second, you're not auditioning for a million-dollar job, you're playing for free so you have nothing to lose. And third of all, just by making it to the Florida State Orchestra level you are in the very top percentage of cello players in the state of Florida. You are already at the top, and even if you are not Number 1, you are still performing better than most, so that means a lot in itself.

Successful people do what unsuccessful people are unwilling to do. They make the hard choices, suffer the sacrifices, and endure the process from beginning to end. They don't wait for their dreams to come to them... they go out and get them. Now is the time for you to make that turning point and make that change in your life.

This is your moment, so make the most of it. Don't wait. Seize the day. Do it now!

Many people never get started on their goals because they fear failure—or because their goals seem impossible. The sheer size and scope of the impending project(s) cause people to feel overwhelmed, and as a result they often don't even know where to start. Many individuals that I've encountered over the years say they don't have any motivation to do anything because it seems so hopeless that anything will ever change or improve. That's very common when it comes to getting out of debt, finding the right relationship, and building a better future. When you're in that position and in that frame of mind, it is extremely hard to see the light at the end of the tunnel. But there's a solution to that problem. It's called Getting Started.

Baby steps are the place to start: teeny, tiny, little bite-size steps that are made consistently and continually. Sometimes this is the hardest part, but consistency is the key to success. Once you start with little steps and start building up momentum, then you will start feeling more confident. You will start feeling the power. Once you get the power, be determined and tenacious to keep going until you finish. Don't quit and don't let anything take you off track.

When I was a child, there was a children's holiday movie called, "Santa Claus is Comin' to Town" that came on every year in December – right before Christmas. One of my favorite songs from the movie has a powerful message that has remained with me for years. The song title is, "Put One Foot in Front of the Other." In the movie, a young Kris Kringle is trying to help evil villain The Winter Warlock to become a nicer person. The chorus says, "Put one foot in front of the other; and soon you'll be walking across the floor…Put one foot in front of the other and soon you'll be walking out the door…" But my favorite part of the song is a verse that makes a lot of sense not only at Christmas, but all year long:

*"If you want to change your direction,*
*If your time of life is at hand,*
*Well, don't be the rule, be the exception*
*A good way to start is to stand."*

Funny, the things you remember and how inspirational a song can be to a young child.

## Analysis Paralysis

Don't get me wrong... thinking about your goals and dreams is a very good thing. It's helpful to weigh the pros and cons; do research to determine the best way to accomplish something; and avoid the mistakes other people have already made. But it's something altogether different to spend all your time thinking just to conclude that something can't be done; or is too ambitious and out of your comfort zone to even consider at all. That is what's called Analysis Paralysis – where you basically over-think an idea to its death; and talk yourself out of moving forward and into staying still.

Remember, "a good plan today is better than a perfect plan tomorrow." Why? Because nobody really knows what tomorrow holds. Analysis Paralysis is that irritating, negative voice that whispers in your ear all the reasons why something won't succeed. It is built on fear, logic, anxiety, and acceptance of the idea that just because something hasn't been done before – it can't be done at all. We all know that's simply not true. I'm sure Analysis Paralysis was front and center, opposing every great mind and inventor that has ever accomplished an amazing feat. Analysis Paralysis is why people thought the earth was flat; why a six-minute mile seemed impossible; and why nay-sayers argued that a person would never walk on the moon. The scary thing about Analysis Paralysis is how highly contagious it is. Once one person gets it, it spreads like wildfire to douse the hopes and dreams of optimistic and ambitious people everywhere. But the cure for Analysis Paralysis is simple: don't believe it. By choosing to believe in yourself, your dreams, and your abilities, you can overcome the source and symptoms of Analysis Paralysis and make your dreams come true.

### Rebel With a Cause

It's time to silence the voices of negativity! Once you get over the negative voices in your head that cause Analysis Paralysis, then it's time to tackle the voices on the outside called Other People's Opinions. Don't let your family, society, friends, or people around you determine your goals, your achievements, or your likelihood to accomplish them. Your goals and dreams must come from your inner heart and soul. If they are not, you won't achieve them anyway. You will just get frustrated and have the illusion of failure, when in fact you were never meant to have those goals to begin with since they were not your own. Also, don't sacrifice your ethics or beliefs to achieve your goals or desires. If they do not align with your true soul, they will be impossible to reach and sustain. You must be true to yourself. You must know yourself, your priorities, your morals, your ethics, and your values. Then you must make sure that your purpose and plan align squarely on the foundation of your principles. I think the Bible states it perfectly: 'What does it profit anyone to gain the whole world and lose their soul?' It's OK to rebel against the status quo. It's OK to do the right things the right way and go after what you really want in life. Be audacious, be different, be bold! Successful people stand out in the crowd, they don't just blend into the crowd. Don't settle for average or mediocre, have a higher standard. Rise above the crowd. Be what others are afraid to be. Dare to dream, and dare to do – be a rebel.

Do you remember the 1950s film "Rebel Without a Cause," featuring bad-boy James Dean and actress Natalie Wood? It was a tale of teenage angst and anxiety. Well, I like to think of myself as a Rebel With a Cause, fueled by my desire to achieve positive success and inspire others to do the same.

I want you to join me as I rebel against the status quo; rebel against mediocrity; rebel against complacency; and rebel against dream stealers. As a rebel, you have the right to live life on your own terms.

There is a lot of value in learning from others who are already where you desire to be. And seeking out professional mentors or advice can help you avoid a lot of mistakes along the way. It's important to always listen, but don't be afraid to be different or to challenge the status quo. And don't be afraid to oppose the crowd and ignore the naysayers who attempt to discourage you.

It is the rebels who stand out, achieve their dreams, and exceed their expectations, because they aren't afraid to take risks. I consider myself a Rebel With a Cause, because although I'm willing to take risks, to take a stand and do things on my own terms, I always want to have an impact and make a positive difference in other people's lives. Not all rebels are rowdy, and not all rebels are wrong. If you have a goal, dream, or belief, then become a Rebel With a Cause and make it happen.

**Information is Your Friend, Never Stop Learning**

Don't ever stop learning. Always seek education. Whether it is an actual school classroom, a seminar, hardcopy books, audio books, learning from others, or finding a mentor – make learning a priority. There is NO EXCUSE not to learn. There is an abundance of free or low-cost education available now with the Internet, seminars, libraries, and all of the technology currently available. If you are looking to learn more about business, research your local SCORE (Service Corps Of Retired Executives) chapter. They have seminars, online classes and one-on-one mentoring services, most of which are free.

There are different ways to learn and everyone learns differently. Some learn best by listening, some by reading or seeing, and some by actively participating. Marketing researchers have determined the process of how most people retain information. From the least to the most effective, most people retain information best in the following order: Read. Hear. See. See and Hear. Discuss. Experience. Find your best way of learning and use it to your advantage.

You can easily find someone who already knows how to do something and is willing to teach or mentor you. The advantage of finding a teacher or mentor is that they have already learned what not to do and learned from their mistakes through experience. I love the quotation that says, "Good judgment comes from experience; and experience comes from bad judgment." Having someone else teach you what to do and which mistakes to avoid can save a lot of time, energy, and frustration.

Sometimes it is good to have more than one teacher because different people have different life experiences. It's true that we can learn something from anyone, so don't be afraid to listen to someone new, someone older, someone different, someone younger, someone who's unfamiliar, and someone who's very familiar with you and your dreams. Don't ever pass up an opportunity to learn from others, because you ultimately learn more about yourself.

Have you ever thought about how much information and education are available for us if we're just willing to take advantage of it? I think about how many resources are available on the Internet with the click of a button, versus growing up with just a dictionary, thesaurus, and a set of encyclopedias. Now, online courses, workshops, seminars, magazines, newsletters, crowd-sourced encyclopedias, podcasts, training manuals, webinars, presentations, and more bring the entire world to our doorsteps, or better yet, bring the entire world to our smartphones.

One of the beautiful things about life is how many places and people we can learn from. I like to consider myself a lifelong learner. That means I don't ever want my education to end. I'm a huge advocate for formal education, continuing education, and higher education. I also believe that there are some things that schools can't teach. Some lessons are meant to be learned by observation, experience, or the school of hard knocks. Some days I think there should be a degree program – or at least a graduation – for acquiring street smarts because school and formal education don't teach you everything you need to be successful in life.

School Smarts is not Street Smarts. Street Smarts is not School Smarts. And book smart is not always representative of real life. How many people do you know who did fantastic in school but could not hold a job? How many people have you heard about who have master's degrees or Ph.D.s but can hardly earn a good living? How many people do you know who did terrible in school, but turned things around and ended up being very successful? Think about the fact that Microsoft co-founder Bill Gates dropped out of Harvard University, and things still worked out pretty well for him. Some of the world's best known and most successful entrepreneurs don't have college degrees. And some people with a whole lot of initials before and after their names live very unfulfilling lives. There are stories about high school dropouts who are very successful and stories upon stories of very educated people who go nowhere. Yes, education is valuable – get as much as you can. But don't discount the experience and drive in somebody with a purpose and a passion. Common sense, real-life experience, education, and knowledge must all be combined to achieve success. Just because someone did well in school does not mean they will do well in life. However, just because someone did not do well in school does not mean they will not be successful. It takes more than education and street smarts to be successful. It takes a combination of things including guts, drive, planning, tenaciousness, common sense, self-belief, and adaptability.

I heard a story about a 79-year-old woman who was conversing with a friend and reflecting on her life, remembering some of her greatest accomplishments and deepest regrets. She spoke warmly about her wonderful husband, beautiful children, and the amazing years they spent together as a family. Then she paused, stating that her only real regret was not finishing college and getting her degree. Her friend said, "Well, it's not too late. What are you waiting for? Why don't you go back to school now?

The grandmother laughed, shook her head and said, "No, it's too late for me to go back. Do you know how old I will be on my birthday? If I go back to school now, I'll be 80-years-old." Her friend stared at her with a puzzled look and said, "Well, how old will you be if you don't go back?" What Are You Waiting For, and Why Are You Still Waiting?

## Go!

*"Where you look, you go!"*

I have a friend whose dad used to drive kids in the neighborhood to school. He was a great guy and a safe driver, but he also used to site-see as he drove. It was funny, because when he passed something interesting, he would look out the window, and wherever his eyes went, his hands—and the steering wheel—went too. I'm sure that made for some interesting and hair-raising rides to school. The point is once our eyes lock in on something, our mind processes it, and the rest of us tends to follow. It's the same way with our goals and dreams. Where you look you have a tendency to go. So, do not look where you do not want to go. Yes, I know that it's hard to not look at the obstacles around you, but that's not where you want to go. Focus instead on the goal ahead so that your mind, body, and actions will follow your eyes.

Another example of this concept is from when I was a union electrician. I worked in oil refineries, nuclear plants, and chemical plants. I had to walk 8-inch I-beams hundreds of feet in the air with no way to tie off for safety at the time. You can ask most ironworkers and they will all tell you the same thing: when you are "walking steel," never look at your feet and never look down. Just walk like you're walking across your kitchen floor and look straight ahead. Focus on what is in front of you, not what is beneath you and around you. If you focus on what is beneath you and around you, it will throw you off and you are much more likely to fall. So you must be laser-focused on what is in front of you and what your intentions are. At that point, my intention was to walk safely across the steel I-beam to the other side, and that's what I did. Set your sites on where you want to go and don't stop until you get there.

There's a concept called the Reticular Activating System – also known as the RAZZ filter. Here's how it works: the basic idea is that once you become informed and focused about a particular topic, then you pick up on its presence and influence more acutely. For example, if you decide to purchase a red sports car, the moment you focus in on that decision, you will begin to notice more red sports cars around you. If you decide to learn to speak Spanish, you will immediately notice more Spanish-speaking individuals around you. Now, when you decide to pursue a particular goal, your brain tunes in and targets the information and resources you need to accomplish that goal. To activate your RAZZ filter, focus on what you really want in life; write it down, state it aloud, recite it everyday, and the things you need to realize that dream will become more accessible to you. Pretty cool concept, huh?

Here's a question: Once you get going, how do you keep going – especially when the going gets tough? Well, there's a secret I use that I'll share with you. I make my goals a game. Sometimes if you make difficult things in life a game and if you turn the challenge of winning into a game, it makes things much more lighthearted, easier to do, and fun. Playing a game often takes the fear and the anxiety out of whatever it is you're trying to accomplish. Since a game is made up, that means you can make up the rules and design them in your favor so that you win. You can give yourself prizes or rewards along the way. You can set benchmarks and deadlines to measure your progress, and you can challenge yourself to improve without the added pressure and expectations of others. Anything that has the potential to overwhelm you can be made into a custom game, designed for you to win. That process creates momentum and a lot of positive energy too that can fuel your progress.

**Jump Into Action**

You can pray all you want, but don't forget God helps those who help themselves. Just praying for something to happen is not going to make it happen; that is why God gave you talents and abilities. Pray for guidance but jump into action.

Your life is waiting for you to live it. Your dreams are waiting to be realized. Your destiny is waiting to be pursued. What are you waiting for?

When I was 14-years-old, I basically blueprinted my life. I decided I wanted to go to cosmetology school to be a hairdresser. At the time, I wanted to make enough money so I could be independent and move out on my own. I had very good grades in high school, and I did not want to go to a trade school during the high school day and miss my classes. At the age of 14, I researched all of the cosmetology schools in the area. I found the one that I was interested in. I rode my bike to the train and took the train to visit the school on my own. While I was there I filled out all the forms and paperwork. Later, I rode my bike to the bank to set up a bank account with the small amount of money I had so I could pay for it each month. Fortunately, my parents were willing to provide the money for the rest of my education. I started cosmetology school full time 40 hours a week when I was 15—the summer between my junior and senior years in high school. Since I did not yet have a driver's license, I walked or rode my bicycle down to the train station and took the train to cosmetology school. When school started in the fall, I attended high school full time and cosmetology school two nights a week and all day on Saturdays. Once I finally got my driver's license in March of that year, I was able to drive to school in my parents' old 1966 beat-up Chevy Impala station wagon with over 165,000 miles on it. I remember I was so grateful to be allowed to drive that old car. Only two weeks after I graduated high school, I finished cosmetology school. Shortly thereafter, I received my hairdresser's license and started working as a hairdresser full time several weeks after graduating from high school. Even as a teenager I made plans, figured out what I wanted to do, figured out a way to get where I needed to go, and how to make it all work. At the age of 14, I knew I didn't want to wait for my dreams to find me, so I went looking for them. It's never too early to start pursuing your dreams, and it's also never too late. It was a long journey from there to here, but I made it in spite of the people who didn't think I could. The lesson I want to share with you is that no matter how you start or where you're starting from, you CAN get there from here.

**Keep on Dreaming**

*"It's not just about the dream, it's about the spirit in which you pursue the dream and who you can inspire and uplift along the way."*

My dreams didn't stop when I was a teenager. No, I had a lot more in store for me beyond graduating high school and becoming a hairdresser. Admittedly, I've made some mistakes and even been sidetracked for a while, but I never lost sight of where I was headed. Just like we already discussed, you must keep your eyes on where you want to go in order not to lose focus. You must turn on your RAZZ filter to attract what you need to get what you want.

In 2002, when I decided as a divorced single mom to move someplace warm, I didn't just simply jump into the car and show up in Florida. I made a plan, a blueprint. After a lot of planning and research, I ended up choosing Florida. I then had to decide what I wanted to do for a living. Because Florida does not have strong unions, I could not be an electrician any longer, since it did not pay very well in Florida to be an electrician. Also, since I now had young children, I needed a position that could be flexible with my schedule. An electrician usually has set hours, and that wouldn't work any longer. I also needed a career where I could control my own destiny and get started quickly. I decided on real estate sales. I went online, searched all the information I could to find out what it would take to become a licensed real estate agent. I found schools, then researched prices and other pertinent information.

Piece by piece, I worked on getting each area of my life organized. The next thing I decided to do was travel to Florida and determine which area of Florida I would prefer to live in. Believe it or not, I bought a fifth-wheel camper, hitched it up to my truck, packed up my two very young children, and for five weeks in the summer while school was out, we traveled around different areas of Florida checking out neighborhoods and school systems. The last place we came to was the Sarasota area. I knew as soon as we got there that it was the place I wanted to be. The school system was great. The beaches and waterfront were beautiful. And the people in the area were friendly. I even drove through the subdivision where we ended up buying our house. I just knew in my gut and by instinct that this was the area and the subdivision where I wanted to live. The children and I went back up to Illinois, sold most of what we owned, sold the house, packed up, and moved to Sarasota County, Florida.

On December 2, 2002, with the thermometer reading six degrees below zero, we left for Florida. We finally arrived after two days of driving. The first thing we did was go and stand out on the beach and watch the sunset;

it was a wonderful feeling to be with my two children hand-in-hand, our feet in the sand, with the warm sun glistening down on us as we watched a beautiful sunset. Two days earlier, we had been freezing our buns off while packing up a moving truck. As the plan continued, I registered my children in the school that I had chosen and realized that I knew absolutely no one when I couldn't even list an emergency contact name on the school's paperwork. After registering the children for school, I registered myself for real estate school and our new life began. Yes, there were fleeting moments of doubt, but not enough to deter me from my dream.

After I passed my real estate exam, I began working for Century 21. After several months, I found a house in the subdivision that we liked. I totally remodeled the house and moved in. Several months later, I went to real estate broker school because in the state of Florida you need a broker's license to own your own company. I passed my broker's exam and immediately started my own company. Within one year I owned my first RE/MAX franchise and within the second year I owned my second RE/MAX franchise. After a few years, my RE/MAX office was the most successful office for production per agent in the entire area—with only 15 agents—while most other offices had more than 50 agents at the time. In 2008, friends of mine who owned other RE/MAX offices in the area made me an offer I couldn't refuse - to buy my RE/MAX offices. Several of our offices combined to become one big office, and we became one big happy family. Through planning and perseverance, I watched my life fall into place.

Looking back, I realize it was a gutsy maneuver to pack up and move to a place where I had no network or ties, but it was part of my master blueprint plan. I knew what I wanted, and I understood the steps I needed to take to make it happen. I was ready for a new start, and I was motivated to make a change. Waiting for my situation to improve on its own was never going to happen. I followed the steps I'm sharing with you and decided to take matters into my own hands. I continue to blueprint my life to this day. This book is part of my current blueprint. One of my goals is to inspire as many people as possible to not squander their potential, but to follow their dreams. If I can do it, you can do it too. What is in my current blueprint? You will have to come on the journey with me, but the best is yet to come, and I can't wait!

## CHAPTER 3

### RESCUE YOURSELF

*"No matter what your past is,
your future can be anything you choose."*

I recently had someone tell me that they wished they were as strong and confident as I am. I told them that I definitely was not strong and confident when I was younger, and there are some days when I'm still not strong and confident. I think that "driven" is a better description of me. I think just having that drive helps build strength. It's the experiences that build the confidence. When you're first starting out, there is no way to really have confidence because you haven't done anything yet. You don't have the life experience to be confident, and don't forget there is a difference between being confident and being egotistical. Being egotistical is not a good thing - being confident is. I think you build up confidence as you overcome obstacles and gain experience. You will never be strong and confident if you don't have resistance and difficulties. It's just like working out in the gym. The heavier the weights you work with and the harder it is, the stronger you get and the more your muscles build. For me, I gained a lot of confidence being the only woman working with all men as an electrician and being able to be successful in that realm. I did things like walking steel I-beams a couple hundred feet in the air. After getting across, I thought, 'holy cow I can't believe I did that', and also 'thank God I didn't fall down and die.' When I ran heavy equipment like cranes, backhoes, skid loaders, fork lifts, etc., it really gave me an adrenaline rush and more confidence. I think the harder and more unusual the thing you do, the more confidence, experience, and the more adrenaline you gain. It is also easy to lose confidence and backslide, that's just a reality of life. When you feel this is happening, it is time to find a new challenge in order to rebuild your mental and emotional muscles, confidence, and strength. Success, results, and accomplishments are the foundation of many people's self-esteem.

One of my favorite quotes ever comes from the famous spiritual leader Dr. Martin Luther King Jr. In his famous "I have a dream" speech delivered on August 28th, 1963 he said, "I have a dream that my four little children will one day live in a nation where they will not be judged by the color of their skin, but by the content of their character."

Those words are powerful and so meaningful. You are not your circumstances. You do not choose where you were born, what color your skin is, if you are male or female, what you're nationality is, etc. What you do choose is who you are as a person, the quality person you are, the quality of life you live, and what you give back to this world. It is all based on your choice and free will. It is all within your own control. Anything that is worth doing is going to be challenging. Don't play small so you can win. Don't play small because it is easy. Give it your all and play full-on. Anything less than that is not even worth pursuing.

Where you start from means nothing, but you have full control of where you end up. It is all free choice and free will. Oprah is a great example. Look at where she started compared to where she is now. Look at Cher and Dolly Parton, where they started compared to where they are now; all of them giving back to others along the way. There are so many stories of people who have such horrible experiences and come from challenging backgrounds, yet they choose to succeed. Why is it that they succeed while others are left behind complaining about the challenging background or horrible life experiences and use that as an excuse just to wither away into another horrible life? From the other side, look at all the people who had all the possibilities handed to them and did not succeed, but rather went down in flames. It is all a matter of free choice and free will. You can choose to cry and feel sorry for yourself and spiral downward or you can choose, and sometimes it is extremely hard, to move forward and grow and succeed.

Famous basketball star and arguably one of the world's best basketball players, Michael Jordan once said, "Some people want it to happen, some wish it would happen, but others make it happen." In the late 1970s when Michael Jordan was a sophomore in high school, he tried out for the varsity basketball team. But standing only 5-feet, 11-inches tall, Jordan was deemed too short to play at that level by the head coach. Michael Jordan could have given up on his dream that day after facing such a crushing blow at such a young age. He could have thrown up his hands and taken "No" for an answer, in light of the initial disappointment. But he didn't. He didn't walk away from the opportunity to play on the junior varsity team instead. Jordan essentially rescued his future career as a world-class athlete by taking advantage of the option to keep playing on some level instead of quitting on all levels. Fortunately for him and sports fans everywhere, he made the right choice by listening to the coach's advice, improving his skills, and increasing his work ethic to a higher level. Personally, I believe that if Jordan had given up on the sport of basketball at that crucial moment in his life, then he would have set himself up for failure throughout the rest of his life. Just like any other behavior, quitting can easily become a bad habit. When life appears to erase your dream, just re-draw it and keep going after what you want. There's no need to wait for somebody else to decide whether or not you can have the life you want. Just because someone else says no, that doesn't mean they are right. You can decide. You can make it happen. You can do it. Spoiler alert:

Don't be surprised if you sometimes have to do it on your own.

Just so you know - Michael Jordan missed over 9,000 shots in his career and lost more than 300 games. At least 26 times he was supposed to take the game-winning shot and missed. He failed over and over again and that's why he succeeds and is known as one of the best basketball players in history. Failure equals success.

## The Cavalry Isn't Coming-
## You Have To Rescue Yourself

Here's a wake-up call: The Cavalry isn't coming, and you can't always call in for back-up. If there is something that you want for your life, now is the time to rescue yourself. Batten down the hatches and hold on tight, because this ride called life is filled with bumps and bruises. Sometimes you will encounter situations where there is simply no one there you can lean on or that is able to pull you out of the circumstances you're in. That's OK, because it is in times like those where we really learn what we're made of and find our own strength and calling and build our muscles.

It seems like some things should be easier than they are. You have a vision, make a plan, and then start working your plan. But we can all agree and witness to the fact that... how shall I say this?... "Stuff" happens.

You build your personal blueprint, decide how you want to live your life, define your dreams, make your plans, when suddenly, while traveling down the road to success unexpected pitfalls and potholes, show up in many forms. From impossible bosses, unhealthy relationships, and dysfunctional family issues, to out-of-control debt, and many other things. Life can often catch you by surprise. When it does, make sure you still have a plan for surprises; expect the unexpected and create a plan of escape to rescue yourself.

When I first got married, I'm sure that my husband and I both believed it was "till death do us part." I honestly don't believe most people go into marriage expecting to get divorced. Some do. But I didn't. When things got bad and then got worse, I had a decision to make. I could keep pretending nothing was wrong, that problems would work themselves out, and that if we ignored things long enough they would get better. That's not how it works. I realized that I could stay and do nothing and watch things falls apart or I could throw myself a rope and climb my way out. So, that's what I did. I rescued myself out of a bad relationship, uprooted from the past and created a new future for me and my children. I am in no way saying that divorce is the right option for everyone; I'm simply saying it was the right option for me. But for many other people, they stay and try to endure, by lying to themselves saying everything will get better. These people come up with excuses to try and convince themselves that this is how life was meant to be. The time is up for making excuses for yourself and other people because we're afraid of risking failure or not living up to someone else's expectations for our lives. But when you're ready to play this game of life full-on, and you've made a commitment to be "all in," then you know that excuses aren't worth the words they're made of, and you need to make a move to rescue yourself.

The term rescue means "to free from confinement." Based on that definition, in a literal sense, you will be called upon to break free and escape from the "prison of your circumstances." Anything that confines you, also limits your abilities to accomplish your dreams. Whether you feel confined by your upbringing, education, finances, family, or relationships, the only way out is up. It's time to move upward and onward toward your goals.

The notion of 'Rescuing Yourself' isn't just a philosophical or motivational one. Due to changes in the economy, lack of funding, budget cuts, you name it... there are scenes playing out all over the country where citizens are being called upon to rescue themselves. Consider this story out of Milwaukee, Wisconsin, where Sheriff David Clarke began airing Public Service Announcements to local residents essentially urging each of them to "rescue yourself." Why? He states that because of budget cuts to the municipality, calling 9-1-1 during an emergency is no longer the best option. In the radio announcement he says, "You could beg for mercy from a violent criminal, hide under the bed, or you could fight back. But are you prepared? Consider taking a certified safety course in handling a firearm so you can defend yourself until we get there. You have a duty to protect yourself and your family." Wow. Talk about the cavalry not coming... that's a prime example.

The beauty of Rescuing Yourself is that you often reap the reward of rescuing some others and bringing them along with you on the journey. Rescuers are heroes. Think about every tragedy or crisis where someone has gone out of their way or put their own life on the line to save another person. They are automatically considered to be a hero. The same is true whether you save a kitten from a tree, a child from a burning vehicle, or yourself from an abusive marriage. The time has passed for looking around and waiting for the hero to arrive. You are the superhero in your life's comic book chronicle. You may not be wearing a cape and leaping over tall buildings, but I guarantee that if you do a close enough inspection of your life, you'll begin to uncover super powers and hidden strengths you didn't know you had.

Even though I've been saying it for over 30 years, I'm not really a big fan of the saying, "What doesn't kill you makes you stronger." I mean, honestly, who wants to go through something that almost kills them? My point is that throughout our lives, most of us will experience great adversity and significant challenges that will ultimately make us stronger and guide us to our destiny. Along the way, our success over those trials and obstacles not only will grant us the freedom we desire to escape the confinement in our lives, but at the same time, it will inspire and encourage some others to do the same. All the world loves a hero, an over-comer, and a great come-back story. My personal inspiration comes from individuals like Ray Kroc, Michael Jordan, Thomas Edison, Walt Disney, Grandma Moses, Aron Ralston, Oprah Winfrey, and others who simply kept going even when it was hard.

**Real-Life Heroes**

American inventor Thomas Edison worked through adversity and persistent failures to accomplish many things in his lifetime. When he was questioned about his failure and success, he replied that he "had not failed, but rather found 10,000 ways not to make an electric light bulb work." I love his perspective – it proves how important having a positive attitude really is. Had Thomas Edison blamed the materials or the technology, and waited for someone else to get his light bulb to work, then the world would have remained darker for a bit longer and it wouldn't be Edison's name that we remember in the history books. Edison also went on record saying, "Our greatest weakness lies in giving up. The most certain way to succeed is always to try just one more time." We should all embrace his advice and make a commitment to see things through and persevere until the end.

I'm inspired by Thomas Edison's story, but I must admit that attempting something thousands of times is a daunting task. I do, however, believe that the ability to persevere and stay committed to a dream is what separates the winners from the non-winners. The ability to keep going is what gets you across the finish line. Momentum is the fuel for a lot of creative genius. The process of stopping and starting and the energy it requires is often the culprit for unfulfilled dreams. Imagine if you were driving at night in a heavy fog that only allowed you to see a few feet in front of you. How far could you possibly make it if you had to stop and start the trip over from the beginning every time you couldn't see what was around the next bend? That wouldn't make any sense at all. Instead, you would slow down and turn on the fog lights, knowing that the fog is eventually going to lift. Some of us need to turn on our fog lights, which may include the resources and support systems around us. Technology is an awesome "fog light." If you aren't sure that you have all the information you need, read a book, take a class, or participate in a seminar to get the knowledge you need to complete the project you're working on. Just don't give up, and don't wait for someone else to do for you when you can do it for yourself.

Rescuing yourself isn't just something that has to occur in a business or professional situation, but it can also refer to a literal, everyday life situation. For example, consider the now-famous hiker Aron Ralston, for whom the movie "127 Hours" was based on during an experience he had back in 2003. For Ralston, the day started like any typical Saturday morning in April where he had planned a routine hike and bike ride through Blue John Canyon in Utah. While he was descending a slot canyon, a suspended boulder he was climbing down became dislodged, crushing his right hand and pinning it against the canyon wall. Ralston had not informed anybody about his hiking plans, so unfortunately, no one would know his whereabouts and no one would be searching for him for quite some time.

Literally wedged between a rock and a hard place (inspired by Ralston's autobiography title) and assuming that he would die, Ralston spent five days slowly sipping very small amounts of water and eating his small amount of food, all while trying to extricate his arm. Sadly, his efforts proved to be futile and ineffective because he could not free himself from the 800-pound stone that was confining his body and limiting his mobility. After several days of trying to lift and break the boulder, the dehydrated and delirious Ralston had enough of the pain, so he prepared to amputate his trapped right arm at a point on the mid-forearm, in order to escape. On the fourth day he realized that in order to free his arm, he would have to cut through it, even though the tools he had available were insufficient to do so. I can hardly imagine the level of "intestinal fortitude" (guts) it takes to make such a monumental decision. But when the reality sets in that no one else is going to make it happen for you, sometimes the only option you have is to rescue yourself.

By Day 5, Ralston had run out of food and water and was forced to drink his own urine to survive and to remain hydrated. He carved his name, date of birth, and presumed date of death into the sandstone canyon wall, and then videotaped his final goodbyes to his family. Deep down, he did not expect to survive the night. After waking at dawn the following day, he performed the amputation, which took about one hour using a dull knife. Aron Ralston not only endured the physical pain of his arm being pinned under a boulder, but also the mental and emotional turmoil of having to make such a life-altering and risky decision. But he realized that if he was going to be rescued, then he would have to rescue himself. That 800-pound boulder was the only thing that stood between him and his freedom. Now, most of us will never be called upon to physically amputate a limb, however, there are some things we may encounter that parallel Ralston's story. We may not lose an arm, but we might be required to sever a friendship or relationship for the sake of survival. Aron Ralston showed a great deal of courage and perseverance and was able to take decisive action when it mattered the most. At some point in time, the same will be required of us. Are you ready to Rescue Yourself?

Too many of us are still full-time victims, blaming someone else for the current state of our lives. It's true that things don't always work out the way we want them to. But like I heard a friend of mine say: If you won't get over it, at least get on with it. It's time to get on with it and rescue yourself. It's time to take back the controls of your life and change directions if you don't like where you're headed. We know that life allows for U-turns or Do-Overs, so take one.

There are too many examples of people who started with nothing—and then achieved phenomenal success—for us to keep making excuses for not having the life we dream of. If you want things to change, change them. I've been there, so I know that it's not always easy. But it's crazy to stay somewhere you don't want to be – hoping someone else will take control of your life and change it for the better. When I was in a bad marriage, I knew it was time to rescue myself, rescue my children, rescue my dreams, and rescue my future. It wasn't enough to just talk about it, I had to put my words in to action. So that's what I did. I rescued myself and my children and we moved to a warmer part of this country. Some of us need to rescue ourselves from mediocrity and make a determination to pursue excellence. Others need to rescue themselves from complacency and the "good enough" syndrome. Why? Because good isn't good enough when you can be great.

I wonder what motivates real-life heroes and trailblazers to want to do something no one has ever done before. Is it a desire to be famous? Are they rebelling against some childhood insecurity? Or is it an internal element that just boils over and compels them to pursue greatness at all costs? Do you have a dream that's bigger than you tucked away inside – just waiting to get out? I do. I have dream to impact the world. I don't simply want to write one book or be on television a handful of times. I want to make a real impact, and not just here in the United States, but across the continent and around the globe. When people hear the name Donna Palm, I want them to say, "Now there's someone who made a positive difference in this world. Wow, I wonder how she did it! If Donna Palm did it, I can do it too!"

Real-life heroes from all walks of life inspire me to dream bigger and to be better. I know—as well as anyone—how easy it can be to accept the status quo or take the easy way out. Sometimes traveling the common, popular pathway is enticing because it doesn't require nearly as much effort. Truth be told, being a pioneer and visionary is hard work. Doing something that no one else has done—risking failure or financial ruin—can seem too daunting a task to tackle. Our inner voice tells us that someone else can or will do what we were meant to do. Our inner fears convince us that we're helpless and at the mercy of our fate. However, deep down there is another truer voice that speaks to us; one that asks us: If not you, then who; and if not now, when?

It takes true grit to Rescue Yourself. However, that is the only way any of us will ever be free.

## "Rescue Yourself"

Here's a brief Rescue Assessment to help determine how you approach responsibility and personal accountability in your life. Remember, it's just an assessment to get you thinking about how you might be able to approach future situations differently to get what you want in life.

|  |  |
|---|---|
| 1. How often do you feel helpless to change your life's circumstances? | Circle one<br>1    2    3    4    5<br>Rarely   Sometimes   Often   ____ score |
| 2. How often do you blame others for the current challenges you're facing? | Circle one<br>1    2    3    4    5<br>Rarely   Sometimes   Often   ____ score |
| 3. Do you make decisions based solely on the input or approval of others? | Circle one<br>1    2    3    4    5<br>Rarely   Sometimes   Often   ____ score |
| 4. Do you make decisions based on how you believe others will feel about or view you? | Circle one<br>1    2    3    4    5<br>Rarely   Sometimes   Often   ____ score |
| 5. Do you feel that people who have been unkind should make amends with you? | Circle one<br>1    2    3    4    5<br>Rarely   Sometimes   Often   ____ score |

| | |
|---|---|
| 6. Do you believe that people who have been unsupportive of your dreams are judging you? | Circle one<br><br>1  2  3  4  5<br><br>Rarely  Sometimes  Often  ____ score |
| 7. How often do you make decisions based on society's expectations of success? | Circle one<br><br>1  2  3  4  5<br><br>Rarely  Sometimes  Often  ____ score |
| 8. Do you think there are too many challenges or obstacles in life to accomplish your dreams? | Circle one<br><br>1  2  3  4  5<br><br>Rarely  Sometimes  Often  ____ score |
| 9. Do you agree that bureaucracy and "red tape" hinder most people's goals? | Circle one<br><br>1  2  3  4  5<br><br>Rarely  Sometimes  Often  ____ score |
| 10. Do you agree that other people should feel obligated to help accomplish your goals? | Circle one<br><br>1  2  3  4  5<br><br>Rarely  Sometimes  Often  ____ score |
| **Rescue Yourself** | TOTAL _____ |

*How did you do?*

A. GO-GETTER. If you scored between 10-17, you are an extremely confident and take-charge person who generally takes full responsibility for your actions and doesn't rely on others to get where you want to go in life. Be careful not to alienate other people by completely dismissing or ignoring their views. You are definitely a Go-Getter, and you aren't waiting on anyone to rescue you.

B. ACHIEVER. If you scored between 18-25, you are definitely a high Achiever. You make intelligent and informed decisions; and based on those decisions, your self-esteem and self-confidence are very high. Like all Achievers, once you get started, you have the potential to produce amazing results – just be sure to keep the momentum going. You are not waiting for anyone to rescue you. Don't get distracted by the dream stealers and remember to remain focused on the finish line.

C. CONTENDER. If you scored between 26-33, you are a Contender. You're in the game, but you're playing by somebody else's rules. Contenders are usually in the middle of the pack; not out front leading, and not in the back straggling - but safely tucked away out of the danger zone where the risk is minimal and there are plenty of others to blame if things don't work out. Contenders can sometimes be indecisive because they factor in so many other opinions and then end up not doing anything. Contenders often fall victim to Analysis Paralysis. It's OK to take a chance to go after your dreams. You're within striking distance of your goals, so don't quit now!

D. PEOPLE PLEASER. If you scored between 34-41, you are a People Pleaser. Unfortunately, your decisions are based primarily on what you think others are thinking about you. The ironic thing about being a People Pleaser is that most people are so busy thinking about themselves, they're really not thinking about you at all, so take back some of the power you've given to others and use it to power your own dreams. There is no need to fear what others might think or judge about you. You have as much of a right and opportunity to pursue success as anyone else. Take some time to refocus your energy on you instead of others, and you'll find that what you want has been there all along.

E. VICTIM. If you scored in between 42-50, you might be a Victim. The danger of being in a perpetual state of victimhood is that your life becomes solely dependent upon the ideas and actions of others. Now is the time to start relying on yourself, and to increase your confidence and self-worth. You are not who others say you are – you are who you prove you are. Don't keep falling victim to the opinions and judgments of others, and don't accept the notion that you have to live your life to meet another person's expectations. Blueprint your life, your desires, and your dreams – and then follow that plan all the way to success. Today is the day that you can begin to Rescue Yourself!

*Dream Bigger, Live Better*

## CHAPTER 4

### WHAT DOES IT TAKE TO BE A SUCCESS?

*"Our greatest glory is not in never falling, but in rising every time we fall."* ~Confucius

Donna, read your own book!

That's the advice I kept giving myself while I was writing this book. From time to time, I would worry about how the project was coming together or get distracted and discouraged because life would get in the way. The advice I gave myself was this: Read your own book! Sometimes all of us just need a reminder of the things we already know. All of the information and ideas I'm sharing with you have worked for me and helped me through tough times; so I know they have value. But even though I know what has worked for me, sometimes I still need a reminder to keep going, even when it's hard.

Yes, we all know that perseverance is one of the keys to success, but we also need to be reminded of what it takes to keep going and what to do when we don't feel like doing it. What I hope you will take away from reading this book is encouragement to keep going, to pursue your dreams, to be the total, complete version of you - fulfilling your greatest potential.

Have you ever noticed how easy it is to get started on something, and how difficult it can be to keep going and finish it? It seems like when we start out, we are fueled by excitement, energy, passion, drive, and anticipation of a great result. Unfortunately, it doesn't take long for reality to set in. The excitement and energy we have quickly fizzle out upon the realization that we still have other responsibilities and challenges that don't go away just because we started something new.

Or sometimes, even when we still have the energy and excitement that propelled us to start, unexpected challenges and obstacles get in the way and slow us down. There's nothing like an unforeseen problem to suck the life out of your enthusiasm.

*Donna Palm*

## Get out of your own way

*"Be Bold and Courageous"*

There's a bad habit I used to have that was preventing me from living up to my fullest potential. I routinely—and sometimes unknowingly—would put myself down or criticize myself or my goals before anyone else could. When it came to stealing a dream, I was my own worst enemy.

Looking back, I wonder how I could let something like that happen. How could I be so confident, successful, and self-assured in so many areas, and then turn right around and diminish my own accomplishments and allow my insecurities to take over? For me, the answer was simple. Life had hit me hard in a lot of different ways and I became weary and worn down. I was overwhelmed with responsibility and the day-to-day grind of juggling a lot of different priorities. Because some dreams had taken longer than I hoped, I had lost faith. Has that ever happened to you?

When I was growing up, my neighbor and very close friend (who was about 20 years older than me) went through a very difficult time in her life. She was a hairdresser. She told me it was a good idea to have a trade so I would always have something to fall back on. She is the reason I became a hairdresser at the age of 16. At the time she was married to a very successful builder who after about 15 years of marriage took a turn for the worse. He started doing drugs, cheated on her with several other women, and eventually lost his business. When they were finally divorced, it left her in financial and emotional ruins with two young children to raise on her own. She had gone from living a very stable and successful lifestyle to having her life turned upside down. In order to stay home with her children she built a hair salon in her basement and worked very long hours in order to provide for them. I was always inspired by her confidence and tenacity. Even on days when she might have felt insecure, you never would have known it because her inner strength was contagious. I learned many life lessons from her. It seemed the harder things were, the stronger she became. As life would have it, several years later she met someone new and fell in love with a wonderful man. They were very happy. She didn't know it initially, but it turned out he was a multimillionaire. They were married and lived "happily ever after." Funny how life turns out sometimes isn't it?

**Believe It**

*"True success is not doubtful or anxious, but confident and at peace."*

If you want to be successful, you have to believe it. You cannot just dream yourself into success. In order to achieve your dreams and goals you must truly believe they are possible. You cannot achieve what you do not believe. If you truly do not believe, it is like a mind-block or wall in your subconscious that you will not be able to pass through.

By declaring something, it becomes a positive statement; an intention which your mind perceives as truth. You have more control than you realize. No matter where you are in life or what the situation looks like, make sure you stay in control of your thoughts and your destiny. I want you to walk through your fear. Once you get past your fears and get over your fears, it creates inner strength and you become stronger than ever. Overcoming fear is like building muscles for your confidence and your mind.

When I was the only female electrician and the only woman on construction sites, it was very difficult. I learned to be very strong. Deep down, I felt like God was training me for something in the future and that's why He was pushing me so hard to make me stronger. I never knew why He was training me but for some reason I just felt there was always greater purpose to it; that He had some kind of plan for me or I wouldn't be doing it in the first place. Being in that environment made me realize that sometimes you have to take other people's opinions with a grain of salt. Everyone has an opinion. It is good to listen to other people's opinions, but do form your own. Don't let other people dissuade you or change your mind if you really feel strongly about something. You may be in training too. There may be a reason things are difficult. There may be a purpose that you do not yet see. If you have no struggles in life you will not build any strength. You may have to determine what advice to take and what advice to leave behind. It is all a learning experience.

## Be Adaptable

*"Nothing is forever - change is the only thing you can rely on."*

Being adaptable, this is one of the most important things to learn. It is all about survival. Of all the things I tried to teach my children, this was one of the most important concepts I hope they absorbed.

Millions of years ago there was a big, strong, ferocious, blood-drinking, carnivorous creature known as the Tyrannosaurus Rex. He was about 40-feet-long about 20-feet-tall and could eat 500 pounds of flesh in one bite. He put fear into the hearts of all the other dinosaurs, being the vicious scourge of a creature he was.

About the same time there was a little six-legged creature, basically known as a pest. This little creature was feared by no one back then and probably ate the remains of garbage and excrement the great and powerful T-Rex left behind. Other dinosaurs probably didn't even notice this tiny little creature, in fact they probably just stepped on him.

Well time went by, the environment changed. The big vicious powerful creature did not adapt, but the little pest did. By now I am sure you can guess where I am going with this story.

It does not matter who or what is at the top of the food chain. If they can't adapt, they die. It is not the biggest or strongest who survive, it is the ones who are most adaptable. That is why to this day those darn cockroaches are still running around adapting to pesticides, laughing at us and eating our food. It is also why you don't see any giant T-Rexes roaming around and terrorizing the city.

The same goes for us. Just remember there are many T-Rexes in the world that will not last. They will have their day in the sun and be gone. Some of them may make a lot of noise while they are here, but don't worry, they won't adapt. So the moral of the story is-

BE A COCKROACH - BE ADAPTABLE

This holds true for everything. Whether it is in your personal life, your business life, your dreams, your plans or your blueprint, you have to be able to adapt. Life changes, environments change. There are many big corporations that were once T-Rexes but have since become extinct because they could not or would not change or adapt to changing times.

You need to be adaptable for any kind of change, even positive change. You need to be ready for growth. Prepare for success so you can handle it tax wise, system wise, personality wise, and in every other conceivable way. There are so many people who suddenly become successful that go off the deep end and lose control either financially, mentally, with drugs, spending all their money, etc. How many stories have you heard of lottery winners who win millions only to be broke a few years later? The entertainment industry is filled with T-Rexes. Don't become successful only to become extinct like the dinosaurs.

You must have change to grow. You must have change in order to achieve your dreams. You must be willing to let go in order to move forward. Don't be afraid of change - Be Adaptable!

*Dream Bigger, Live Better*

## Pop That Bubble

*"I Know Help is Out There, But I Can't Seem to Get to It!"*

Have you ever felt trapped? Lost? Lonely and just can't seem to get out of the "poor me" mentality? Have you ever felt like you were inside a bubble? You feel like you can see out and you know there is help and support out there, but you just can't seem to reach it or remember how to find it? It's like there is a giant bubble surrounding you and you see everyone you know out there but no matter how hard you scream for help it seems that no one can hear you. You try to pick up the phone but you just don't know who to call. The bubble blocks all communication. Your mind just draws a blank because you are so into the funk you just cannot even think clearly. We are all trapped "in the bubble" sometimes. We need to know how to find the pin that will pop the "Bubble."

Everyone's pin is different. Everyone needs to find their own pin before they get stuck in the bubble. For me, I've found over the years that when I am trapped in the bubble, calling other people or being surrounded by other people really helps. But I notice when I am really stuck, I can't even think of who to call.

Ironically, everyone has so many people in their lives that sometimes we forget them. How many times have you visited with a friend or family member whom you haven't seen in years? You get together, have a wonderful time, and it never fails when you go to leave everyone says they should get together more often. But, alas life gets in the way and it just doesn't happen. Sometimes those are the best people to call for inspiration. You might want to make a list—with contact information—of family, friends, or even support groups. That way when you are lost "in the bubble" and you can't think of who to call, you have a tangible list, with contact information conveniently in place. Make the list before you get into the funk. As you think of or see people, add them to the list. Think of positive people, ones who can lift you up and out of the funk. Try to avoid negative people because you don't need to have anyone joining you in the bubble that doesn't have a pin to help you get out. Undoubtedly, there will be several people on the list that you never would have thought of calling when your mind is blank; many times those are the people who will inspire you the most and who have a pin in their pocket that they will happily share with you so you can pop that Bubble!

## Be 100% Responsible

You choose your own perception. You are responsible for what something means to you. Be 100 percent responsible. You can control how you perceive things. Sometimes it is difficult. You can be optimistic or pessimistic. You can be negative or positive. You can choose what things mean to you. This creates your life. You can perceive things as success or failure.

In relationships, you are 100 percent responsible for your experience within the relationship. Don't fall for the 50/50 concept. It is simply not true. Each of you in the relationship is 100 percent responsible for your own experience. Do not play the blame game. If, for example, you feel your partner is not living up to your expectations or not treating you as you feel you should be treated, realize that you are 100 percent responsible for staying in the relationship and choosing your experience. You are 100 percent responsible for whether you communicate your needs and expectations. If your partner chooses not to meet your needs or expectations, that is 100 percent their choice, and it will be 100 percent your choice as to whether you accept that.

This holds true in all areas of life. You choose. Be 100 percent responsible. I realize there are some things that happen beyond your control. However, how you choose to react and respond to the situation is 100 percent up to you.

## Perception Is Reality - Or Is It?

*"We cannot change anything if we cannot change our thinking."*

You create your world. Your beliefs and perceptions are how you see and feel your world. You often create your world just by what you say and believe or perceive. This can be positive and negative. For example, if you say something is scary, that is your perception. It is your belief. Something is not necessarily scary; it's your emotional creation of it. You create what you say and you believe what you say. For example: I'm not good enough, it's hard, this is overwhelming, etc. If you changed what you say to 'I know I can do it, this is easy, or we can get this done with no problem,' you just changed the entire paradigm of your perception as well as your entire experience of life.

Don't forget there is a difference between scary and uncomfortable. There is also a difference in actual physical danger and just being scared by your perception of something.

Your perceptions and beliefs can change your entire experience of life, especially if you have a paradigm shift. A paradigm shift is like an epiphany or an "aha, I get it" moment. I always use the example of a prism. If you look through a prism in one direction, the color of the light may appear blue, however if you turn the prism in a different direction, the light may appear red. A paradigm shift is the point of change. This example is not exactly scientifically accurate but I am using it as an example for explanation purposes. I am using the term "paradigm shift" in the context of a complete change in perception. Your perception is created by your view of things, your previous experiences, and the filters you see your world through.

I challenge you to Walk on Water. Impossible? Not really. When we are willing to think differently, our possibilities can change. When we make the effort to open our minds, we can literally change our lives.

Let's get back to Walking on Water and making the impossible possible. If you only think of water as a liquid, you will not be able to walk on it. However, if you allow your mind to expand and think about changing the structure of the water to a form that supports you, then suddenly walking on water becomes possible. Freeze the water and it will allow you to walk on it with little to no effort.

Just by changing the composition, surroundings, the parameters, and the expectations, we can make the impossible possible.

Valerie Daniels-Carter is one of the best-known fast-food operators in the United States. In 1982, Daniels-Carter, along with her brother Attorney John Daniels, started V&J Foods with a single Burger King restaurant. Within 16 years, she nurtured the company into a 137-unit, multi-brand operation. She now sits on several national boards. Even though Valerie has never played or coached professional football, she sits on the board of directors for the National Football League's Green Bay Packers. When the players on the field were successful in earning their Superbowl rings, all of the board members (who play and serve in a different capacity) earned their Superbowl rings too. Never say never. Most people would think it's nearly impossible to earn a Superbowl ring if you aren't a world-class football player, and almost everyone would agree that it's impossible for a female entrepreneur to earn a Superbowl ring. That's only true if you think the way everyone else thinks. Once you change the paradigm of your thinking, anything and everything becomes possible – even winning a Superbowl ring (without getting tackled on the gridiron).

Advertising and marketing companies use the art of perception constantly. Marketing and perception is everything when it comes to advertising. In marketing and perception, it is not about whether something is real or not, it is what people perceive as real that matters. It is a very interesting conversation. Is reality perception? Or is perception reality? What is real?

No matter which side you take, the reality is that your perception of everything is what creates your life experience and who you are as a person. Think about it.

## Sometimes You Just Have To Prove Them Wrong

Not long after I moved to Florida and earned my real estate license, I went to work for the local Century 21. It was my first experience in real estate sales and I was still learning the ins and outs of the business. At the time I drove a 2000 Ford F-250 4-Wheel Drive Crew Cab Diesel truck with over 200,000 miles on it (I purchased it new and still drive it to this day). The first broker/owner I worked for insisted that I sell my truck and buy a 4-door car in order to take clients out to show homes. He said, "You will never make it in real estate driving a truck." I love my truck and I was not willing to give it up. Time went on, and this broker started getting very insistent that I buy a 4-door car and actually became verbally abusive about it by trying to embarrass me in front of the other agents at office meetings by ridiculing my truck. I just decided at that point I would have to prove him wrong. I could sell real estate while driving a big truck. To make a long story short, I became one of his top agents; and the day I earned my brokers license (about a year later) I left and started my own business - all while still driving my truck.

Within one year I owned my first RE/MAX office and the following year I owned a second RE/MAX office. I still drove my truck. In fact my offices became much more successful than his and at Realtor meetings or wherever else I saw him I always mentioned that I still drove my truck. I used to laugh to myself and enjoy proving him wrong. In fact it wasn't until I sold my RE/MAX offices that I bought another car, keeping my truck of course. Sometimes the best way to prove someone wrong is to be successful, smile, and never say a word.

**Getting Past Limiting Beliefs**

Dealing with excuses: What's my excuse? What does my excuse give me permission to do or not to do? If I could no longer use this excuse what would I have to do instead? Why don't I just do that now?

Sometimes self-imposed excuses are just a safety net. People who make excuses also tend to downsize their dreams. For example, if you started and then quit pursuing your college degree, the next step in your thought pattern might sound something like this: "Well, I've been successful without a college degree, so there's no use in going back to school to get it now." While it may be true that you've been successful without a degree, it's also true that you've made an excuse and downsized your dream to cover it up and camouflage the fact that you gave up on a goal. If getting a college degree was your dream, you should still pursue it regardless of whether you need it or not in your current line of work. Following through on priorities sets a strong precedent for establishing the kind of work ethic and commitment you'll need to accomplish all of your goals. Here's another one: "I wanted to lose 15 pounds so that I could fit into my swimsuit on vacation, but I'll just purchase a larger size instead. Plus, it's natural for someone my age to gain a few pounds—especially with my work schedule and especially after having children.

At my age, no one is going to be looking at me on the beach anyway, so I might as well eat whatever I want and enjoy myself – losing the weight can wait." Hmmm, sound familiar? I know I've said some of those things, and I'm guessing many of you have too. Let's agree right now that making excuses and downsizing our dreams is no longer an acceptable practice for our lives.

After a while, it's easy to give up on a dream because it seems so unlikely to come true. Plus, we reason that our dreams are the stuff that fairy tales are made of – and life is no fairy tale. When you stop hoping and believing, you start settling – and no matter what it is, you'll always get less than what you settled for. I want you to make a commitment to keep your dream alive, just the way you dreamed it; just the way you imagined it; and just the way you want it. Don't downsize your dream because of how improbable it is. Remember that it is the vision of your soul that breathes life into the realities of your dream.

You can live in your small world of excuses or you can live fully in an unlimited world. What is it that challenges you and would cause you to go a little bit farther, dig a little deeper when times get rough? What are you willing to work for day and night? What challenges are you willing to overcome so you can get to the prize at the end and live the fantastic fulfilling life you have always wanted? In order to follow your dreams you must get past your usual limiting belief system. You have to push past what you believe are your limits.

Imagine if you are a handsome Golden Retriever. Your greatest joy in life is running free through the yard with the breeze flowing through your golden hair. You see in the distance a beautiful white fluffy Standard Poodle; she is beautiful and you are in love. You want more than anything to go meet her and romp in the grass. As you run in her direction, ZAP! You suddenly get a painful shock around your neck. You stop in your tracks. You try again and ZAP! You get shocked again and run back with your tail between your legs. The invisible electric fence is holding you back from your dreams. You are limited to your yard, never to reach your true love. You pace back and forth, you see the love of your life a short distance away - she is looking at you with her big brown eyes beckoning for you to come play. What do you do? Is your dream worth the pain?

Finally you decide to take a fast hard run at it. At full speed you run straight for your dream, ZAP! Yes, the fence gave you a good sting, but you just broke past your limits through the next yard and are heading straight for your dream.

Sometimes it may sting to break out of your comfort zone and past your limiting beliefs, but it is the only way to achieve your dreams.

## Levels Up - Getting Comfortable With Them

There is a difference between being uncomfortable and unsure and real fear. Don't wimp out because you are uncomfortable. To be successful and grow, it is worth being uncomfortable or in unfamiliar surroundings. Many people don't succeed because they don't believe they can succeed and because they are not comfortable around success. For example if you are used to driving an old beat up car and then suddenly you take a brand new, very expensive sports car out for a drive there can be a feeling of "uncomfortableness" – or discomfort. It may just be because of the difference or it may be because internally you feel you do not deserve or feel comfortable around the high-end vehicle. In order to move up to the next level, you must feel comfortable at the next level. For example, on the golf course the old saying is you play better golf with better golfers. But when you first go out to play with the better golfers there is discomfort and nervousness, or possibly a feeling of not belonging. After several rounds this slowly goes away and a sense of belongingness or deservedness is created. You now are starting to feel comfortable at the next level.

The same goes for people. Imagine the feelings of others who have traveled up the ladder of success. In the beginning they may have come from very humble backgrounds and had difficult life experiences. I am sure as they started moving up the ladder there were plenty of times that they felt uncomfortable with their surroundings or the people around them. They simply adjusted, became comfortable, and moved up the ladder. The irony is that now they may be at the top and many people feel uncomfortable around them because of their success. I am sure when many of them were young and just starting out they could not have possibly imagined that people would feel nervous around them, as they had felt uncomfortable on their way up the ladder.

The moral of the story is you must not only believe in yourself but you must learn to be comfortable in surroundings at the level you would like to achieve. It might be a good idea to spend some time in these areas. Whether it is financial success you are looking for by spending time in high-end stores or test driving high-end cars in order to feel comfortable with them, or if you are trying to move up a level in your career, start building relationships with people at that level. Possibly through work experiences, seminars, mentoring, or other possibilities you can meet and relate with people at the level you would like to aspire. The idea is to be comfortable and build confidence with the people and surroundings at the level you would like to be.

## Strive for Excellence, Not Perfection

*"Perfection is an illusion"*

Because there are no perfect people, there also are no perfect plans; no perfect marriages; no perfect parents;

no perfect children; no perfect businesses; no perfect ideas; and no perfect paths to success. I am going to give you permission to be human and fallible. Understand this: perfection is not a standard for which we should strive, however excellence is. Why? First, the goal of perfection is unobtainable and therefore, destined to end in failure.

It's time to "UN-DO" some things and let go of some habits that we've picked up along life's journey. I don't know for sure where this originated, but early on, it appears that most people fall into the trap of trying to be something they are not and never will be – perfect in someone else's eyes. Little girls desire to be the perfect angel for their parents. Little boys aspire to perfection in sports and athletics. Teenagers attempt to be the perfect friend to imperfect acquaintances and associates, which frequently leads them down the wrong path. Students strive for perfect grades, drowning themselves in stress, drugs, or unethical methods to obtain them. For those young adults who consistently fall short of that measure of perfection, life becomes a self-fulfilling prophecy of let-downs and failures that often lead to future sub-par performances.

Now, don't misunderstand me. I don't want to be mediocre in anything I do; and you shouldn't want to be mediocre either. But I don't desire perfection, because I know it's not going to happen, and the stress that it creates to pursue perfection is not worth the cost. Although there may be perfect moments that culminate from the right timing, training, preparation, and opportunity converging at once, there are no perfect lives that can remain indefinitely and consistently perfect.

There are four reasons why perfection should not be your goal. Perfection is-
1. Unobtainable
2. Unsustainable
3. Unrealistic and
4. Unforgiving.

**Unobtainable** – By establishing perfection as the goal, we are basically setting ourselves up for failure. To pursue an unobtainable objective ultimately undermines our plans and decreases the likelihood that we'll continue making progress because we know we'll never realize success. Realistically, how many people can keep running a race that has no finish line? That's the equivalent of chasing perfection.

**Unsustainable** – On limited and rare occasions, some of us may have experienced perfect moments that represented the right time, place, and opportunity for success, but we'd also have to admit that it was short-lived. We hear celebrities and entertainers talk about a perfect performance or perfect production, but we rarely hear of perfect seasons; perfect days-yes, but not perfect months or years. That's because perfection is not sustainable – it cannot and will not last long.

**Unrealistic** – Would you even want a perfect life? For as much as we hate trials and challenges, truth be told, they make us stronger and better. I have a feeling that experiencing only sunshine without any rain, or only good things and never pain, would make us unable to appreciate the life lessons we need to survive, grow, and thrive. Living a perfect life is a fantasy and it's an unrealistic expectation. The best thing each of us can do is to expect the unexpected, prepare for every opportunity, plan for the worst, but hope for the best.

**Unforgiving** – When we keep falling short of perfection, it begins to take a toll on our confidence, our self-esteem, and our ability to believe in ourselves. We cannot be successful in an environment where we feel we can never win. Consistent and repeated failure is the guaranteed result when we chase an Unobtainable, Unsustainable, Unrealistic, and Unforgiving goal. I want to encourage you to toss out the ideal of perfection and pursue excellence instead. If you keep moving in the direction of what you want, you will continue to get closer to what you desire. Even when I felt like I was a million miles away from accomplishing my dreams, I knew that if I just kept moving toward them, one day I would open my eyes, look up and see them in the distance, clearly within my reach.

**Be Tenacious**

*"When you have exhausted all possibilities, remember this – you haven't."* ~*Thomas Edison*

In terms of excuses, I've got more than most. But I made up my mind early that I would not allow any of my circumstances (adopted as a baby, married and divorced as a young adult; homeless for a while; female entrepreneur; single parent; victim of the recession and economic downturn, and on, and on, and on...) to stand in the way of my success.

It concerns me to think about how close I might have been to accomplishing some of my goals, had I simply kept going and given it one more try. Although most of us don't hit success on the head the first or second time, nobody really knows whether it's going to be the fifth, 10th, or 100th time when it all comes together and works out the way we hoped. Think of all the things we wouldn't have if the innovators, authors, and entrepreneurs had simply given up after the first few attempts. If Thomas Edison had quit working on his inventions after the first three times, instead of the 10,000th time, we wouldn't have light bulbs, batteries, or the engineering processes that eventually led Henry Ford to advance automobile production and manufacturing processes. We would not have epic works of literature or mesmerizing artistic masterpieces. We wouldn't have email, Disneyworld, or the theory of relativity. How you view success and failure makes all the difference in how you will approach situations that require you to keep going - even when it's hard.

During a motivational session, I once heard a speaker ask the following question: "What would you do if you knew you couldn't fail?" Have you ever thought about that before? What would your life be like if you whole-heartedly gave 100 percent to your ultimate goals and dreams – without the distraction or the deterrent of fear interfering with your progress?

Too many of us waste time trying to walk a perfect path to success – as though making a mistake (or several mistakes) equates into automatic, irreversible failure. Well, I for one, reject the idea that there are any perfect pathways. As a matter of fact, oftentimes the process of learning from your mistakes is the path that will lead you where you ultimately want to go. Think about how much more we could get done if we weren't so concerned about doing everything perfectly the first time.

What goal would you pursue whole-heartedly if success was guaranteed? I imagine that most of us would take it to the limit and go 100 percent, full-out after everything we ever wanted or ever imagined that we wanted.

To quote hockey player and coach Wayne Gretzky, "You miss 100 percent of the shots you don't take." A loss is only really a loss if you quit, because quitting ends the game and makes the loss final. Trying again keeps the game going and gives you another shot to win. Call it a failure or a loss, but as soon as you decide to give it another go, the game automatically goes into overtime.

Let's be honest: many people simply are not willing to do the work that it takes to get what they want. Whether it's paying off debts, being healthier, or improving our relationships, it takes what it takes to get what we want. You must be tenacious, whatever happens, no matter how hard it is, don't quit on your dreams. Just do what it takes to get to where you want and just enjoy the ride. Think of it as a roller coaster. There will be times when you are going uphill and it will be hard and it may be scary, but then there will come the thrill of going over the hill spinning around with the wind blowing through your hair - and the fantastic feeling of freedom and confidence when you finally let go and fly.

## What It Takes

**Confidence** – I once heard it said that Confidence is the most important attire you can put on. When it comes to confidence, we should wear it like a custom-tailored suit. Somehow, confidence has the ability to mask our flaws and deficiencies and re-direct attention to where we want it to be. Think about a time when you've encountered a confident person; suddenly the name-brand clothing and expensive labels didn't matter as much because you knew the person had what it took to get the job done. Strong confidence can powerfully overshadow the attributes that might detract from us. Confidence and a smile are a winning combination when dealing with people to close the deal, get the contract, satisfy customers, or get what you want out of life.

**Like-Minded People** – It is absolutely true that one rotten apple spoils the whole barrel. Amazing how that works; that the unhealthy and unproductive aspects of one thing can infest and infect the other things that surround it. Attitudes work like that too. It only takes one negative nay-sayer to derail a plan and diffuse a dream. Negative people can suck the air out of a room or drain the life out of an idea faster than you can say, Yes We Can!

**Blueprint Plan** – We've already covered this topic extensively, but it's worth repeating, because having a solid plan that outlines your vision and details what you want and where you want to go is extremely important. Your Life Blueprint represents the schematic design of the life you desire. The plan dictates to you and to others what needs to be done, what skill sets are needed, what talents are useful, and what education or experience is required to accomplish your goals. Not only does the Blueprint tell you where you're going and how to get there, but it also tells you who to bring with you along with way. That's an important factor because the right people at the wrong time will be ineffective, and the wrong people at the right time will be useless. Timing is crucial.

**Perseverance** – It takes a lot to keep going, especially when it's hard. Perseverance is that characteristic that makes us reach down deeper, dig in our heels, and make a determination that quitting is not an option. No matter how hard or hopeless the situation appears to be, we will not accept NO for an answer; in essence, we will not be denied that thing we are working toward or believing for.

**Faith** – When we hear the word "faith" we often think of God, higher beings, divine inspiration, or spirituality. Faith can be all of those things, some of those things, or none of those things. In and of itself, faith is simply a trust in or reliance on and hope in something. We can believe and have faith in ourselves, our talents and abilities. We can also believe and have faith in things outside our control. When we bestow our trust upon another person or object, we put our faith into that entity – with the hope and belief that they or it will meet our expectations. It is important that we also have faith in ourselves and a strong sense of belief that we can make our dreams come true.

**Resilience** – It's absolutely necessary to be resilient and hopeful in order to be successful. You must be resilient in the face of challenges and be self-aware of your own thoughts; and the little voice inside your head must continually coach you toward success. Resilience is that unwavering ability to bounce back, even after you've been hit hard. It's the internal rubber ball all of us need that simply keeps on bouncing back no matter how hard the blow or how intense the trial. Things that are resilient can take a pounding and yet retain their form. That's how we need to be. When life strikes, we simply need to snap back into shape... and keep on going.

**Success Secrets**

After much consideration, it seems to me that if there was one single secret to success, we would all know it by now. After all the books, workshops, seminars, presentations, and motivational speeches, certainly the secret should have been revealed by now. So what I've realized is that there isn't just ONE secret, there are several so-called secrets in addition to a series of steps that lead us down the path headed toward success. Since there is no one prescribed method, we can learn from the journey of others, avoid their mistakes, find new and interesting ways of doing things, follow our hearts and passions, and still end up in the place that we desire to be. Life is very forgiving if we will simply keep going. That means that on our way from here to there, we will be presented with countless opportunities to veer on and off the path, to make mistakes, and to take a do-over if we need it. But the race is usually won by the individual who makes a blueprint of his or her dream, and then steadfastly sets out on a course to achieve it.

# CHAPTER 5

## RELATIONSHIPS MATTER

In today's modern world, our lives revolve around relationships. Whether it is our relationships with ourselves or our relationships with others, now more than ever our world has become interdependent. With the advent of the Internet, the creation of social media sites, as well as Internet-based television, the people of the world have the ability to communicate and be in relationship now more than ever. People from all over the world can now be in contact both by voice and video anytime, anywhere, almost instantly simply by sitting in front of a computer or holding a smartphone in their hand. There are political and commercial alliances, groups, and organizations all over the world promoting global communication and relationships. Our ability to communicate and be in healthy relationships is the cornerstone of our world.

## We Must Start With Ourselves

*"People notice how you treat yourself –
when you respect yourself, you respect others."*

We are our own foundation. If we don't treat ourselves like we deserve to be treated, no one else will either. If we do not have healthy minds, healthy bodies, and healthy attitudes we will not be of use to anyone, including ourselves.

In order to be successful, in order to make a difference, in order to have clarity and an enduring strength, you must put yourself first. I don't mean that in a selfish way. If you don't maintain your car by changing the oil, repairing the brakes, giving it regular maintenance, and filling the gas tank you won't get too far. If you don't take care of yourself by getting enough sleep, eating healthy, and getting regular exercise you will not be working at your peak performance level. You cannot achieve success if you are run down and not working at your highest potential.

A perfect example is the oxygen mask on an airplane. On every commercial flight as a part of the safety demonstration, flight attendants explain if there is a loss of pressure in the cabin you must put your oxygen mask on first before you help anyone around you, even children. This is because if you run out of oxygen you will be of no use to anyone else. It is the same in life. If you are worn down, if you are not in peak health, if you are stressed, you are not in peak performance. Your ability to perform will waiver. I personally am guilty of this, as well as many other single mothers—and probably most of us—who don't put ourselves first. Throughout our lives we are taught to think of others first. This is totally understandable and is meant to be thoughtful of others. We feel guilty if we put ourselves first. However, it also makes perfect sense that if we are not in our best condition, we will not be able to give back to others or perform at our best level. We must learn to take the time to take care of our health and ourselves - physically, mentally, and emotionally.

## What You Think About, Comes About

*"You must think clear positive thoughts."*

Self-doubt is a natural thing. Everyone doubts themselves. Even the most powerful people, though many just don't show it. Don't play the game of success based on your feelings. You have to play past your feelings. Michael Jordan was not always laughing and having fun on the basketball court yet he learned to play full-out. He was the best because he played past his feelings. You don't think he wanted to play all of the time especially when he was sore, tired, or injured - or everyone else was out having fun and he was still practicing do you?

Have you ever felt like you were trapped; or caught in some sort of emotional vacuum or hole? The key is to be able to pull yourself out of "the hole," which sometimes can be very difficult when you're in "the hole." Even outside sources can cause you to go into "the hole." Life experiences, hormones, medications, and other outside influences can cause you to lose faith, confidence, and your ability to envision your dreams and possibilities clearly. That is just part of reality and life. Just know you will have days like this. Life is not perfect and smooth all of the time. It is just like working out in the gym and working your muscles hard. If it was easy you wouldn't be building any muscles. It is at these times you build strength and inner confidence. This is a very good time to go back to your gratitude list, it will help you realize in your darkest times the positive things in your life and can propel you out of the darkness and out of "the hole" and into the greatness of your own possibility, dreams, and future.

When you're at the bottom it is very hard to even dream of being at the top. Your self-esteem may be at an all-time low. You may not even be able to focus on where to start, as you are so totally lost. I have been there too. And you can be there more than one time in your life. There could be times when you are becoming very successful, and then something causes you to crash and burn and you're back at the bottom again, starting all over. That's life, don't let it discourage you. Remember, you are building muscles.

There are so many examples of comeback stories in our world. There are countless people who were at the top, fell back to the bottom and came back to the top again.

Steve Jobs from Apple was forced to resign from his own company. Talk about rejection. After leaving Apple he did some other computer development not readily considered successful. Later he bought the company which eventually became Pixar, home of many modern-day computer animation films. Several years later, Steve Jobs sold Pixar to Disney and became the largest shareholder in Disney with 7 percent ownership. As we all know, eventually Jobs made a comeback to Apple, restored it from near bankruptcy and developed the iPOD, iPHONE and iPAD. With his technology the world of electronics was changed forever.

The story of J.K. Rowling is also inspiring. The author of the Harry Potter series went from living in poverty to being a multimillionaire in the course of 5 years. During the process of writing, J.K. Rowling endured the passing of her mother, a miscarriage, domestic abuse, a very difficult divorce, surviving as a single unemployed mother, clinical depression, and a contemplated suicide. At one point she saw herself as "the biggest failure she knew." How do you think she felt when she was "in the hole?" What do you think it took for her to pull herself out and continue writing? When the first book was complete, it was rejected by 12 publishing houses. After enduring all the pain in her personal life and then being rejected professionally, what do you think was going through her mind? Where did she pull her inner strength from? Even more of a twist to the story, it is said she owes much to the 8-year-old daughter of the publishing house chairman who read the first chapter and demanded to be able to read more, therefore intriguing her father as to her interest in the book. Life works in mysterious ways.

In his early days, Walt Disney had major financial setbacks including losing the rights to one of his popular cartoon characters. He was over $4 million in debt by the 1930's (imagine how much that would be by today's standards). Disney barely had enough money to complete "Snow White and the Seven Dwarfs," the first-ever full-length feature animated film. The movie became a blockbuster. By taking a chance on something that had never been done before, Walt Disney not only became a huge success, but his first full-length feature cartoon pulled him out of bankruptcy, started the Walt

Disney Studios in California, and of course led to everything that followed: Disneyland, Disneyworld, every other Disney movie ever made. The fact that he didn't give up has affected millions of people, maybe more. Imagine how much joy has been brought to children due to all of the movies and amusement parks. Imagine all of the people who earn their living due to Disney films, Disney television, theme parks, and resorts. Imagine how many people and companies now rely on them to create incomes for their families by selling food, creating novelties, working in the parks and resorts, developing entertainment, and on and on. The number of people affected worldwide is hard to fathom. I think you understand what I am trying to convey. All because one person did not give up on his dream, it steamrolled into affecting millions of people in a positive way.

These three people alone, by not giving up even when they were at their lowest point, have affected millions of other people's lives. How many lives might you affect?

Don't think just because these people are famous and have heroic stories that they didn't have the same feelings that we have when we are at the bottom. Don't ever think that they weren't depressed, feeling hopeless, lost and wanting to give up and quit. The reason they became successful again is because somehow they pulled themselves out of it and did not quit. Don't quit on yourself. Study your blueprint, follow your dream.

OK so you had a difficult childhood. You grew up in a dysfunctional family. Or maybe you suffered from abuse or addiction. I'm sorry, but join the club, so did most of us in some way, shape, or form. Those types of situations can be devastating, with a long-lasting impact. However, you cannot live in a permanent state of victimhood and expect to lead a successful or prosperous life. You only have one shot at life, do you really want to spend it in a "poor me" world? You are not the only person who's faced tough breaks in life. And no matter what it is you have experienced, you are not the only one. You're not the first and you won't be the last. If you won't get past it—because life is a choice—at least get on with it. Time doesn't stand still; times a-wastin'. Now pick yourself up and let's get going!

If you need inspiration all you have to do is search. There is always going to be someone with a more difficult situation than you who pushed beyond it and fulfilled their dreams. So what is your excuse? Get going. If you need some inspiration just do some research and follow someone who inspires you.

Start to think... what inside me is holding me back? What is limiting me? What if my efforts ended up affecting millions of people? Raise your own standards and push yourself a little harder because this increases your self-esteem, especially when you achieve more than the average person would have. Make yourself do what you need to do or should do even if you don't feel like it. Yes, I know from personal experience, this is just plain hard. Do it anyway.

Your goals need to be authentic to your deepest needs and desires, not society's standards. Your purpose in life is what brings you joy and makes a difference in others' lives. Is someone else's life better because they know you? How do you impact others and inspire them? Are you making the world a better place?

Pay attention to your gut instincts, this is different than your feelings. Instincts are intuitive, feelings are emotional. Don't second-guess your intuition. Remember in school they always said when taking a test: go with your gut feeling, it is usually the first answer you give and it is usually the correct one.

Be resilient and positive. If you use up all your energy merely surviving, you won't have any energy left for creativity and growth. In order to be successful you must be resilient in the face of challenge. Be self-aware of your thoughts and that little voice in your head. You must coach yourself in your own mind.

## Inner Strength and Self-Talk

*"Whatever you think causes the way you feel, the way you feel causes the way you act, and the way you act causes your results."*

As I said earlier, your personal self-image can make or break you. All your successes and accomplishments as well as your failures and disappointments start from the inside. Harnessing your inner strength is extremely important when it comes to success.

When you are at the ultimate bottom or having your ultimate struggle, the thing you have to reach for is your inner strength. That is the key to getting over that edge and being strong, confident, powerful, and successful.

Sometimes one of the hardest things to do is to keep an eye on your self-talk. Your self-talk can either bring you down or bring you up. Pay attention to that voice in your head. Try as hard as you can to get rid of the negativity.

Just think of the self-talk that must be going on in athletes' minds as they are playing to win a game, run a marathon, or doing the Ironman after being completely exhausted swimming, biking, and running all that way. They must have an amazing self-talk to keep themselves going to get themselves across the finish line. Think of the concentration and positive thoughts a professional golfer must have in order to sink that putt, with millions of dollars riding on it. That kind of inner strength and self-talk is what we need to be able to get to where we want to go. Negative self-talk will do nothing but destroy you. This is easier said than done.

Try not to have negative thoughts or negative self-talk, especially about yourself. A lot of success is mental and your mental processes in your mind are your foundation. Many people have great success using meditation to help control their self talk and their mindset. Although it can be difficult, you must be able to control your thinking.

You can either be dominated by your commitments and successes or you can be dominated by the emotions and self-talk that takes you out of the game. Don't let negativity dominate you. Allow positive energy, positive emotion, and positive self-talk be your dominant conversation.

You can gain clarity and perspective when interacting with people, so get out and talk to someone positive. Find a mentor. Finding your inner strength is the key. Sometimes you need help from outer sources to get that inner strength.

This is a great time to go back to your blueprint. Go back to your gratitude list. Go back to your list of Whys and Who you need to be to get to where you want to be. Read everything you wrote back when you were all excited about making your plan. Go back to all the positive things you wrote about yourself. This is your truth. This is what you need to study and truly believe. This is what will get your head straight when you are feeling down. This is your instruction manual. Believe it and follow it.

## Being Alone

*"Sometimes good things come apart,
so better things can come together."*

Don't be afraid of being alone. There is peace in being alone. There are so many people out there who are afraid to be alone because they don't know who they really are and what they can accomplish on their own. The problem is when we only rely on others to validate our worth, we never realize our own worth and validate our existence in this world. You cannot define or measure your value in terms of someone else. Each of us must realize our own possibilities and fulfill our own potential. No one else can do it for us. I encourage you to spend time with people who challenge you to grow, rather than those who reinforce your insecurities.

So many recently divorced individuals latch onto the next person that comes along whether it is for a paycheck or because they are afraid of making it on their own. Don't be a "latcher." If you never learn to be on your own and stand on your own two feet, you will never learn what is possible for you. You will limit yourself. You need to be on your own to realize your own possibilities. Also, it is not fair to the person you latch on to because you are not with them for the true reasons you should be with them. No one should be an enabler. If you are an enabler, it is just as unfair to you as it is to your partner for the same reasons.

In my opinion, Integrity is one of the most important traits in the world that a person can have. It trumps money, power, and fame – because there are a lot of rich and famous people who have no integrity and as a result, don't have the respect of others.

The combination of true power and leadership is not something that is forced. It is something that is created and followed due to possessing integrity and respect. A person of integrity warrants a great deal of power and respect.

Surrounding ourselves with the right people has a lot to do with how our lives will turn out. It seems like as we get older, meeting and making new friends becomes rarer. Maybe it's because we are set in our ways and unlikely to meet a lot of new people who fit perfectly into our friendship mold. Or maybe it's because as we get older, we also get more cynical and less trusting –

and don't allow new friendships to develop as easily. I would caution you to choose your friends wisely because the people you most closely associate with are a very good indicator of where your life is going and where your future is headed. I once heard a single friend say, "I'd rather be alone than in bad company." That is so funny to me. Unfortunately, many of us make the mistake of remaining in bad company to avoid being alone and lonely. But those two things are not the same. There are a lot of lonely popular, married, or successful people surrounded by fans, children, co-workers, colleagues, and acquaintances who still feel absolutely isolated, entirely misunderstood, and completely alone. Many people will join us along the journey of success, so it is imperative that we have the right people on the road with us. There will be days when the path is crowded and days when it feels like we're walking alone. The secret is to take advantage of the comfort and counsel of others, while appreciating the solace and solitude of going it alone.

Pack light and move quickly. Don't drag the emotional baggage of your past into the next phase of your life. It will only slow you down and weigh you down. Everything you need is already waiting for you at the point where destiny meets desire.

Don't be dependent on other people. Dependent means that you are dragging someone else down. According to the dictionary, the word dependent means you're reliant on or at the mercy of someone. Instead lift others up, be a source of energy and inspiration.

All of us are capable of many things and sometimes it is great to be reborn and take a do-over whether it is our career, our relationships, or our entire life. Change can be good. Sometimes we need a kick in the head in order to see that we need change in order to grow to a higher level. Sometimes we get too comfortable in life and become complacent wasting our possibilities by not even trying them. We only live one life and we should use it to our full potential.

### Redefining Failure

In my own life I am learning to redefine some terms that have limited me in the past. I don't like the word failure, because it infers that we stop trying and moving forward when we don't instantly get the outcome we want. When my two children were learning to walk, I didn't consider it failure when they crawled first. I didn't consider it failure when they fell more than once in their quest to transition from infants to toddlers. The perceived failure would have been in suspending the process of teaching them to walk because they didn't get it just right the first time they tried. The failure would be in thinking they could never walk because it didn't happen immediately. True failure would have been in refusing to continue the learning process and practice of walking because it seemed hopeless. However, both of my now teenage children are healthy, happy, and well-adjusted young adults who walk just fine. Part of that reason is because we didn't give up and call their initial inability to walk a failure. Success is a process and a journey; failure is only part of the equation when we quit before success arrives. Don't shortchange your life because you are afraid to fail.

Ask for help. Create relationships. It is who you know plus what they know that can add up to great success and be of great help to you. Have peace in your decisions, follow your instincts, be happy where you are now in your life, but look forward to the journey ahead.

When I was a teenager I used to babysit for my neighbor. She had three little girls. There was something she told me that I will never forget and I would like to share it with you. She always told me that if she had a choice between taking her girls to the zoo or cleaning the house, she would take her girls to the zoo. She told me that if she was ever lying on her deathbed, she would regret not spending time with her girls as they were growing up, but she would never regret not having a clean house. In other words, know your priorities. People and relationships are much more important than looking good.

## Relationships With Others

*Communication and Relatedness*

One of the common traits of successful people is that most of them are very good communicators. They know how to speak well, connect with their audiences, and they tend to be very good listeners. These individuals have made a habit of not only hearing what others have to say, but also of processing, internalizing, and utilizing the information when appropriate.

To effectively communicate, successful people also know how to speak to people's listening. In other words, they recognize that communication not only relates to what is said, but how it is said, and most importantly how it is heard or perceived by the person listening. Communication is only as good as perception, because perception is reality. Let's make it a priority to perceive how other people listen and interpret our words and actions; and then be aware of how we can more effectively communicate with them.

Just as important as speaking and listening to what is said is the ability to hear what is left unsaid. Sometimes the information you really need to know is in what is left unspoken. Occasionally, in order to do this, you will need to get past someone's story. People can get wrapped up in their emotions, their story, and what is going on. Sometimes you have to get past that to see what is unsaid. You have to get down to who people are as a person rather than all the baggage that is surrounding them. Sometimes people get wrapped up in their circumstances and you have to be able to see past their circumstances to who they really are.

Communication—at all levels—is one of the keys to becoming successful at any endeavor. Business and journalism schools all over the nation and all around the world remind students to know their audience. It's no different in life. We must understand who we're talking to and why we're talking to them; and then communicate on their level in a vocabulary that's familiar to them. In other words, Communication by the speaker is only as good as Perception by the listener.

Many times when we are upset it is because of a miscommunication or an unmet expectation. It is possible that we just expect that others should know what we want or understand what we need. That just isn't so. We need to be clear in our communications and expectations in both what we want and need as well as what others want and need. You will be surprised how many upsets can be avoided by clarity.

I think another very important point to make is our connection to people; our relatedness to people. In my life I have always been with an extremely diverse group of people at different times. I think in order for there to be a connection or relatedness you should try to relate to people on their level. Not in an artificial way, and not in a way you are not, but more as a way of adaptation. For example, when I sell real estate, if I am working with a farmer, going out to cornfields, I wear jeans and work boots, drive my truck and speak on the same level with the same language, word structure, etc. as the farmer. This creates better communication and relatedness on the same level. I am not being artificial because this is really a part of who I am. When I am working with very high-end luxury home buyers, I dress very professionally in a business suit and drive my Mercedes. I speak at a different level using different vocabulary. My language and mannerisms are different as I am relating to different type of people. This is not to say one group of people is better than the other because that is not true. It is just that different people communicate in different ways. This creates a comfort level for both the clients because there is relatedness. Once again, this is not me being artificial, it is just a different facet of who I am. This goes back to being comfortable in different scenarios with different types of people of different types of backgrounds. This also creates people being comfortable with you as well and points of commonality where we can connect.

## We Are All Just Human

*"Sometimes people are tempted to take the path of least resistance."*

Be generous, but require that people have skin in the game or they won't stand on their own, and they will take things for granted. There is an old saying: If you give a man a fish, you feed him for a day. If you teach a man to fish, you feed him for a lifetime. I know some people think this saying is controversial; however, I am a strong believer that it is true. People have a tendency to follow the path of least resistance. Require people—especially children—to work for what they want or they won't appreciate what they have. That is how we end up with spoiled people and spoiled children.

In my high school there were a lot of very wealthy students. Many of them were given brand new cars for their sixteenth birthdays. My family, as well as most of my friends' families, were considered middle class. Even in high school I made the observation that most of the wealthy students who were handed a brand new car for their sixteenth birthday did not really appreciate what they were given. Most of their cars were wrecked or damaged within the first few months they received them. Those of us who were allowed to drive the family car, most of them "old beaters," really appreciated that we just had something to drive. We had a tendency to take very good care of our vehicles even though they would be considered "old beaters."

If people do not learn how to work for things or have skin in the game, they will never be able to do it on their own or stand on their own. They will take things for granted the rest of their lives and expect to have things handed to them. That doesn't mean you shouldn't be generous and helpful, it just means they should have skin in the game.

**Good Intentions vs. Being Your Word**

Over the years there have been people who have come into my life that are people pleasers. They mean well and they usually have good intentions, however they make promises and don't follow through. Many people serve out of insecurity and can't come through with their promises. They make promises to make people happy, but are never able to keep those promises no matter how hard they try. Most do not have any ill intentions, however be aware so you are not disappointed.

If you have a tendency to just try to make people happy or have the intention of keeping your word, but never seem to be able to, your commitment must be stronger than your excuses. Honor your word and keep your promises. Clean up your broken promises, admit your fault, and clean up your mess. That is what honoring your word is all about. By doing this you will feel much better about yourself and create credibility. Go beyond others expectations, don't make promises you can't keep.

## Consensus Reality vs. Experiential Reality

Consensus Reality, also known as Agreement Reality or Social Reality is a very strong force in our lives. Most people don't even realize that it exists yet it affects us every single day. While Experiential Reality is defined as the reality we experience or learn in everyday life such as hunger, thirst, pain, fear, etc., Agreement Reality is defined as beliefs that are shared by a social group by general consensus. Sometimes these beliefs are correct and sometimes they are not.

There are many things that are real only because society agrees they are real. A basic example is money. A paper twenty dollar bill is only worth twenty dollars because we all agree it is worth twenty dollars. In reality the paper itself is probably only worth a few cents.

The world is full of agreement reality. Most advertising and marketing is based on agreement reality. If you take a certain diet pill you will have a sexy muscular body. If you wear a certain cologne, women will throw themselves at you. If you use a certain skin cream you will become young and beautiful.

In the past, Agreement Reality included the concept that the earth was flat; something Columbus set out to prove incorrect, even though people of his day told him he would fall off the edge. The Wright Brothers transcended the Agreement that if God meant for man to fly he would have given him wings, by achieving flight.

A good leader can break through agreement reality. A great leader can create agreement where there isn't any. Mahatma Gandhi, Nelson Mandela, and Abraham Lincoln spent most of their lives creating their own Agreement Reality while rejecting their society's version of the concept. As you can imagine, Agreement Reality can be a very powerful concept both in a positive and negative way. Be aware. Which side of the reality are you on? Are you leading in the right direction? Do you have the courage to make a stand in the face of no agreement? Do you have the courage to stand up for what you truly believe? Are you ready to be a Rebel With A Cause if necessary? From now on keep your eyes open and notice how many beliefs are really just a Social Reality and not a true reality.

One person's truths and realities may not be another person's truths and realities. We all see the world through our own filters and past experiences.

Unfortunately sometimes Social Realities can become self-fulfilling prophecies. Sometimes when children or teenagers—or even adults—are given a label such as underachiever, troublemaker, etc.- they may live up to that label even though it was not initially part of who they are, but because they start to believe it. If you have been labeled in either a positive or negative way, is it affecting your true belief in who you are?

Don't just exist throughout your life believing what others have labeled you - be committed to living a successful life; a life you choose and design. If you really want to do something you will find a way, if you don't you will find an excuse. Don't make excuses and don't let others make them for you.

**The Eagle and The Chicken Story**

There are many versions of this age-old story, some with happy endings and some with sad. This version just seems to fit here.

Once upon a time, near a large mountainside there was an eagle's nest with three large eagle eggs. One day, an earthquake rocked the mountain causing one of the eggs to roll down to a chicken farm, located in the valley below. A mother chicken found the egg and accepted it as her own. The eagle egg eventually hatched with the other chicken eggs and a beautiful eagle was born. Being chickens, the chickens raised the eagle to be a chicken. The eagle loved his home and family, but in his heart, his spirit cried out for more. One day, the eagle looked to the skies above and saw a group of mighty eagles soaring. The eagle cried, "I wish I could soar like those birds." The chickens roared with laughter, "You cannot soar like them. You are a chicken and chickens do not soar." The eagle often saw the other eagles soaring up above, dreaming that he could be like them. Each time the eagle shared his dream, he was told it couldn't be done. The eagle learned to believe what everyone else told him to be true. After time, the eagle stopped dreaming and continued to live his life as a chicken. Finally, after a long life as a chicken, the eagle passed away never enjoying his ability to soar. The moral of the story is: don't fall into agreement reality. You become what you believe you are. If you ever dream to become an eagle, follow your dreams, not the words of chickens.

## Everyone Counts - Everyone is Important

Have you ever been to an event or a meeting that very few people attended? Many times the only reason it is under-attended is because those invited thought "it doesn't really matter if I don't show up, no one will notice if I am not there anyway." What happens when everyone makes the decision that they don't count, or that they don't matter, or that they are not important enough to make a difference? Exactly, there is no one left. There is no one at the event. Imagine being the event coordinator and no one shows up. Not because it is a bad event, but because no one thought they mattered. It happens all of the time. Everyone matters. Remember the saying "No man left behind"? That is because everyone matters.

In business, I always tell all my employees to please always share their ideas with me because I am always open to new suggestions. Who knows, they may have a great idea that I missed or something that I never would've thought of. However I always tell them since I am the one who is responsible for the company and I am the one who has to pay the bills, I am the one who has to make the final decisions. Everyone Counts, Everyone Matters.

Be a person of contribution. Be a person that when you meet someone and you go to leave, they feel empowered, full of energy, and have a belief in their own greatness. Encourage others. When you put positive energy into other people, not only are you creating success for them but you are creating success and positive energy for yourself and hopefully the world.

*Dream Bigger, Live Better*

## CHAPTER 6

### TIME IS OF THE ESSENCE

*"There is a big difference between activity and accomplishment."*

If you are like me and most people today, you are overwhelmed with too much to do and too little time. There are never enough hours in the day. Just as you finish one thing, something else needs to be done. You may always feel like you're behind the eight ball and will never get caught up.

Especially with all the technology available today that was originally designed to lessen the workload; it seems to have instead created more work and less time. The amount of information that is available is overwhelming. Now more than ever we need to be very selective as to how we spend our time. Sometimes this is very difficult, but we must be intelligent in the use of our time. This means there must be even more planning involved.

We must be efficient in the use of our time executing as many activities and actions as possible without getting stuck in the quicksand of time-wasting activities. Many people make big plans but never get any results due to poor planning or wasting time. One of the best feelings in the world is completing a task and checking it off your to-do list. You will notice the more you get done, the more you feel you can do. Building up momentum is the key. It feels good when you can accomplish things, and when you accomplish things you want to do more.

Always do first the things that will get you the biggest results, especially if it is the most difficult. Choose the most significant task first. If you don't have the time to do it all, make sure you get the most important ones done. Time is more valuable than money; you can make more money, but you cannot make more time.

Here is a cute little story about time and timing. When I used to work at an animal shelter outside of Chicago, I had a very sweet experience. Our shelter used to only try to accept younger animals so we had a higher rate of adoption. One day an old beagle slipped through the cracks and I felt so bad for her because I thought she never had a chance in the world for adoption. Everyone that came in seemed to want younger animals. She was very old, overweight, and waddled slowly. We put her in the first kennel as you entered. Later that day a little old man walking with a cane came in looking for a pet. It turns out that he had just become a widower after having recently lost his wife after many, many years of marriage. He was very lonely. He could barely walk without his cane. As he walked through the door the first dog he saw was the old overweight beagle. He pointed with his cane to the dog and asked, "Can I see that dog please?" I said, "Of course, why don't you go sit in the lobby and I will bring her out to you." I still remember it was so sweet. The little old man sat on the oversized chair. I did not even put a leash on the old dog since she was so slow she could barely walk, but yet she had the energy to waddle out to this little old man and actually jumped up in his lap and curled up and went to sleep. It was a match made in heaven, the little old man who'd been so lonely, had found the little old dog that didn't have a chance in the world. He adopted the dog and they both slowly waddled out the door together, hopefully living happily ever after. I guess it just goes to show even if you're at the end of your life or the end of your run there is always hope for happiness. And when all else seems hopeless there may be some joy just waiting for you somewhere. After all, what were the odds of this little old man being able to find an animal that would be calm enough to live with him, and what were the odds of this little old beagle finding someone who would want a dog who was so old and slow? It was perfect.

## Balance Your Life

You must be able to balance living in the moment, living in the past, and living in the future. The past is over. We need to learn from the past but not dwell on it and not live in it. We need to be prepared for the future and plan for the future but not be obsessed with the future. Many of us who are very success oriented and very driven live so much in the future that we miss out on the present. We must enjoy the present, because all we really have is now. Live in the present in order to succeed in the future.

## The Butterfly

One day while walking in the park, a man found a cocoon that contained a butterfly nestled neatly in the crevice of a tree branch. For several days during his daily walk, he passed by, peeked at the cocoon, hoping and waiting to see the butterfly emerge. One day a small opening appeared at the end of the cocoon. The man sat down nearby and watched the butterfly for several hours waiting for it to squeeze its body through the tiny hole. After struggling for hours, the butterfly stopped and appeared to give up on its quest to leave the cocoon.

Confused and unsure about this process, the man decided to help the butterfly – after all, it was the least he could do to help something so beautiful come into the world. He carefully took the cocoon in his hands and widened the hole so the butterfly could escape. In no time at all, a beautiful butterfly emerged from the cocoon, but it had a swollen body and shriveled wings. The man continued to watch it, expecting that any minute the body would contract, and the wings would enlarge and expand enough to support the body. But it didn't happen. In fact the butterfly spent that day and the rest of its life crawling around; never able to fly.

What the man in his kindness and haste did not understand: The restricting cocoon and the struggle required by the butterfly to get through the opening was a way of forcing the fluid from the body into the wings so that it would be ready for flight once that was achieved.

Sometimes struggles are exactly what we need in our lives because they prepare us for what's coming next. As long as it was housed in the cocoon, the butterfly didn't need wings. But once it was time to leave the cocoon, the struggle is what it needed in order to fly. The lesson of the butterfly—and for all of us—is that going through life with no obstacles or challenges would ultimately cripple us for life. We will not be as strong as we could have been without the cocoon and the responsibility of getting out on our own. Without the struggles, we would never fly.

## Success is a Choice

*"You only have so many hours a day, so use them wisely."*

The life you have now is a result of the choices you've made up to this point. Every choice we make has a consequence; sometimes good, sometimes bad, sometimes neither.

Success is not the same for everyone

That's because lasting success is a series of choices; a lifestyle built upon patterns and behaviors that routinely result in positive, uplifting outcomes. If that same individual succumbs to some type of addiction and ends up homeless or destitute, we reassess his successfulness because his choices are no longer leading toward success.

I encourage you to develop successful habits instead of successful moments. A moment is fleeting and doesn't last. A habit is ongoing, predictable, and sustainable. In order to make your life a successful one, the choices you make should consistently align with success.

I once read that, "The road to success and the road to failure are almost exactly the same." It's not that successful people haven't experienced tragedy, failure, or disappointments. The difference is that successful people turned the negatives into positives; used stumbling blocks for stepping stones; and learned to grow from problems instead of run from problems. Winston Churchill said, "Success is walking from failure to failure with no loss of enthusiasm." If we consider the idea that in terms of success, attitude is equally important as ability, then it becomes clear that success is an equal opportunity, regardless of gender, background, ethnicity, or income. Certainly, the path may seem more clear and the line straighter for those with a head-start who are born into a successful business or surrounded with resources; however there are plenty of people with lots of opportunities—but no ambition—who end up accomplishing nothing. Ultimately, success is about the choices we make.

## Success is Worth the Wait

There are no coincidences in life. You are where you are, facing what you're facing, and doing what you're doing because life is preparing you for future and continued greatness. Don't deny yourself the opportunity to be everything you were created to be. Don't deny yourself – or the world – the benefits from the full potential of your life.

No one can be 100 percent all of the time. Keep this book and your notes as a handy reference. Use it as an instruction manual for your life. If you are not at the top of your game or you feel like you are in "the bubble" or falling into "the hole" refer back to whatever information in this book may inspire you, refer back to it as often as it is helpful. Look back to your notes to be re-inspired and re-motivated. Study your Blueprint. Be re-inspired by your Gratitude list. Go back to your Accomplishments list so you can see written proof of what you have achieved so far. On days when you feel stupid for making the same mistakes again, go back to your Self Improvement list to prove to yourself that you have learned from the past; sometimes it just takes more than one time around.

The intention of this book is not just to read it once but to be able to go back and use the information as often as possible. Life is complicated and most things you cannot learn the first time around. Sometimes you have to repeat the class (or in this case), just repeat the book or the part of the book that will you will find helpful.

This book is a combination of innovative new concepts along with tried-and-true messages and beliefs that have been used for years. It is the best of both worlds. In combination with each other, the intent of this book is to inspire you to get moving and fulfill your dreams. Share it with others so they can fulfill their dreams too.

We were created to fulfill great plans, accomplishing huge tasks, solve big problems, and dream big dreams. Most importantly, we have the ability to bring our dreams and visions to life and to inspire and encourage others to do the same. Each of us is limited only by the belief we have in ourselves.

Blueprint your dreams. Open your mind. Find the answer to What's Your Why? Then go forth and dare to dream, and dare to do.

A powerful quote frequently shared in motivational and leadership seminars states, "Growth happens when what you know changes what you do." So, now that you have more education, information, experience, and a solid Blueprint Plan to follow... what will you do now?

Saying yes to something you previously said no to will alter the course of your life. Responding to an old situation in a new and different way will change the results

When faced with what appears to be failure, we all can make a choice. We can accept defeat and allow the perceived failure to define us, or we can embrace the process of learning; grow from our mistakes and simply try again. At the end of the day, it is still a choice. Choose to follow your Blueprint.

**Go, follow your dreams and live a big life!**

## That's A Wrap

I would love to hear your feedback, success stories, and how this book affected you and improved your life.

I'm always interested in hearing other people's stories because I derive so much hope and inspiration from how successful people get to where they are. By sharing your stories you can inspire others to follow their dreams and provide support for others who are in similar situations.

I also think we should celebrate those of us who are considered everyday people, those of us who are not necessarily the rich and famous. Those of us with everyday jobs and everyday lives; all of us who have overcome tough times and still found a way to stay positive, overcome adversity, and persevere, even when life is harder than we hoped it would be. Everyone counts, everyone matters. We all depend on each other. Success does not always amount to fame and fortune. Success includes being a great parent, employee, or just making the world a better place by being here.

Who would have thought: from scooping poop in kennels and driving an old beater station wagon, to being a cashier in a 24-hour convenience store and being homeless, to being a hairdresser and owning my own salon, to wearing a hard hat and work boots in oil refineries, running heavy equipment and driving a big 4-wheel drive truck, to being a RE/MAX owner wearing expensive business suits carrying a designer computer bag and driving a luxury convertible, to writing a book and working in television. Follow your dreams...

This book is finished... onto the next dream,
the best is yet to come!


www.DonnaPalm.com

*Dream Bigger, Live Better*

Life Blueprint • Journal • Notes

*Donna Palm*

Life Blueprint • Journal • Notes

*Dream Bigger, Live Better*

Life Blueprint • Journal • Notes

*Donna Palm*

Life Blueprint • Journal • Notes

*Dream Bigger, Live Better*

Life Blueprint • Journal • Notes

www.ingramcontent.com/pod-product-compliance
Lightning Source LLC
Chambersburg PA
CBHW060515100426
42743CB00009B/1331